LA BOUCHE CREOLE

La Bouche Creole

Leon E. Soniat, Jr.

Illustrations by Marlene Bettale

PELICAN PUBLISHING
New Orleans

First printing, January 1981
Second printing, March 1981
Third printing, November 1981
Fourth printing, February 1983
Fifth printing, February 1984
Sixth printing, July 1985
Seventh printing, September 1987
First hardcover printing, May 1990
Ninth printing, February 1995
Tenth printing, August 2006
Eleventh printing, July 2010
First paperback edition, June 2022

Library of Congress Cataloging in Publication Data
Soniat, Leon E.
  La bouche Creole.

  Includes index.
  1. Cookery,Creole. 2. Cookery, American—
Includes index.
Louisiana. 3. Louisiana—Social life and customs.
I. Title.
TX715.S67834   641.59763   80-23178
ISBN-13: 9781455627110

Printed in the United States of America
Published by Pelican Publishing
New Orleans, LA
www.pelicanpub.com

Jacket illustration by Marlene Bettale

To Memere, my grandmother, and Mamete, my mother, two incomparable Creole cooks whose cooking was an expression of their love. You'll get to know them in the pages that follow.

Contents

Acknowledgments

Those without whose help this book would not be possible? At the top of the list is my very good friend and wife, June. Her tolerance, editorial assistance, and practical wisdom made my task so much easier. Special thanks also go to my daughter, Yvette (Missy), who hour after hour typed, corrected, and arranged; Margaret Ashley, my secretary, whose help and advice proved invaluable; Rachel Daniel, *Times-Picayune* food editor, who had enough faith in the "Creole Kitchen" to see it become a reality; and Marlene Bettale, who labored long and hard on the wonderful drawings you will enjoy throughout the book. To them all: "You all are beautiful people."

And thanks, also, to the rest of my family—who willingly and sometimes unwillingly were my samplers—Eleanor, Jerry, Leonard, Oliver, Cathy, Chris, Deb, David, Nan, and grandchildren Jerry, Terry, Joel, Timmy, Marcus, Jeanne, Colin, and Russell.

soups &
gumbos

Memere, my grandmother, used to say that the recipe for Creole cooking started with the French love of, and skill in, manipulating anything edible into a tasty dish. Then, if you combined this with the Spanish gust for piquancy, the native African ability for developing a slow cooking method to perfection, and the gift of herbs and spices from the Indians, you had the beginning of Creole cooking.

Now, add a well-seasoned cast iron pot with a nut brown roux; in this pour finely chopped onions, celery, and peppers. From here you could branch out into a thousand different directions, and still wind up with a Creole culinary masterpiece.

All of the recipes in this book are Creole classics. The masters responsible for creating them were renowned for their ability and skill to develop dishes that stroked, soothed, excited, and flattered the palate of even the most exacting Creole gourmet. It is my sincere hope that you will not merely imitate these recipes, but will allow them to serve as a starting point, so that your own personality and creativity will shine forth in every dish you serve. Memere stoutly maintained that the only way one could fully enjoy Creole cooking was to have "la bouche Creole," the Creole mouth. Mamete, my mother, went a step further, with her contention that you also had to have "la boudin Creole," the Creole stomach. So between the two of them, they pretty well locked up the enjoyment of good food exclusively for the Creoles. But, of course, it is well known that anyone can enjoy Creole cooking. This is attested to every day in the fair city of New Orleans, where visitors come from all over the world to indulge in and enjoy our culinary delights.

Let's start with a Creole gumbo, a dish which originated in La Belle Nouvelle Orléans. A gumbo is something unique to the Creole cuisine that developed out of the specialties of this area. One of the greatest of these, actually termed the king of the gumbos, is GUMBO Z'HERBES, the gumbo of herbs or green gumbo. It was traditionally served on Good Friday. It seems that after so many days of abstinence and fasting during Lent, observed in the predominantly Catholic community, one needed the sort of revivification or rejuvenation given by this conglomeration of greens.

To get all the necessary greens, one had to go to the French Market—and what a wonderful place that was! Well do I remember early in the morning, almost at daybreak, how we would set out, for we lived within walking distance of the old French Market. When we got to the vegetable stands, where we bought the ingredients for the GUMBO Z'HERBES, there would be the vegetable men or hawkers and their cries of "Get your greens, lady, get your twelve greens, get your fifteen greens, get your seven greens"—the numbers changed as we passed by each of the different stands.

Legend had it that for every green that was put into the gumbo, a new friend would be made during the succeeding year. And Memere and Mamete, being warm-hearted and gregarious people, would put in as many greens as they possibly could, knowing full well that in the following year they would make that number of friends.

This gumbo also could be served on other Fridays, when we could eat no meat. Nowadays we have improved the gumbo with the addition of a few things. So, let's begin by making the best of the Creole gumbos.

GUMBO Z' HERBES

1 pkg. frozen spinach
1 pkg. frozen mustard
  greens
1 pkg. frozen turnip greens
1 pkg. frozen collard greens
½ cabbage, shredded
2 qts. water
stick butter
2 onions, chopped
1 cup chopped celery
1 cup chopped bell pepper
2 tbsp. oil
1 lb. stew meat, cut into
  small pieces
¾ lb. ham, cut into small
  pieces

4 cloves garlic, chopped
1 bunch shallots, chopped*
4 bay leaves
1 tsp. basil
1 tsp. powdered thyme
⅛ tsp. allspice
⅛ tsp. cloves
½ cup chopped parsley
¼ tsp. Tabasco
5 tbsp. flour
salt and pepper to taste
1 doz. oysters (optional)
filé (if desired)

*When the Creoles refer to "shallots," they mean green onions or scallions. I have frequently used the traditional term "shallots" in this book.

Into the water place the spinach, turnip greens, mustard greens, collard greens, cabbage, bay leaves, basil, thyme, allspice, and cloves. Bring to a boil, lower the heat, and let simmer, covered.

In a frying pan melt ½ stick butter and sauté the onions, bell pepper, and celery. When limp add to the greens. In the same frying pan, fry the stew meat and ham in the oil. When brown add to the pot. Let this mixture simmer for 1 hour and then add the green onions (shallots), parsley, garlic, Tabasco, salt, and pepper. Mix well.

At this point, if you wish you may take about a quart of the gumbo out of the pot and run it into a blender to puree it. Return it to the pot. Now allow to simmer for another 2 hours.

About ½ hour before the gumbo is finished, take the ¼ stick of butter (at room temperature), add to it the flour, and work it into a paste.

When the paste is smooth, slice a bit at a time and add to the pot. The lumps will soon disappear as you stir.

Five minutes before serving, if you wish, add the oysters and their water. Cook until the edges of the oyster begin to curl.

The gumbo is now ready to serve over rice in soup bowls. A pinch or two of filé powder may be added to the gumbo in the bowl, if desired. Serves eight.

Some of us are under the delusion that the Women's Lib movement is of rather recent origin. Not so, dear reader. The beginning of the development of Creole cooking started as a "petticoat rebellion" around 1722. The French "jeune filles" that had come over to Louisiana to marry the settlers were very unhappy. Their problems weren't marital, but rather dealt with food.

You see, those gals were good French cooks, but in Louisiana they were stymied. None of the cooking ingredients with which they were so familiar could be found in the colonies; the major food source was Indian corn. They wanted to go home!

Bienville, however, had a very smart housekeeper, Madame Langlois. It was this French Canadian lady who was finally able to pacify the irate "bonnes femmes". To solve the problem, she organized the first cooking school in America. The French girls were taught how to concoct delicious and interesting dishes with the materials at hand. Madame Langlois taught them how to grind the detested "maize," or Indian corn, between stones to make cornmeal, which was then fashioned into cornbread and served with wild honey. She also showed how to make hominy and grits from corn, and how butter beans and corn combined to make succotash. She demonstrated how to broil, roast, and stuff young squirrels and rabbits. Since seafood was so plentiful, she showed them many ways of fixing fish, shrimp, and crabs.

She also introduced them to filé (fee-lay), which became a favorite of Creole cooks. Filé was an herb given to the Creoles by the Indians; the Indians used it for seasoning as well as for medicinal purposes. It was prepared by taking young, tender sassafras leaves, drying them, grinding them into a fine powder, and then sifting the powder through a hair sieve. I don't know the medical term to describe the physical result of filé, but, in simple language, "it makes you sweat." After downing a plate of hot filé gumbo, one might think that it's the hot gumbo that has made the perspiration flow so freely. Credit for at least part of that reaction goes to the filé.

Filé literally means "to make threads," and anyone who has misused this seasoning knows very well how appropriately it was named. Filé has to be added at the very end of the cooking process—not boiled in the gumbo—because it gets thready or gummy. When gumbo has had filé added to it, it is not a good idea to reheat. The results are usually disastrous.

CHICKEN SAUSAGE GUMBO

1 large chicken, cut in
  pieces
5 tbsp. oil or lard
6 tbsp. flour
2 large onions, minced
1 bell pepper, chopped
1 cup chopped celery
3 cloves garlic, minced
1½ lbs. andouille or
  smoked sausage
2½ qts. chicken stock

½ tsp. thyme
3 bay leaves
⅛ tsp. powdered cloves
⅛ tsp. powdered allspice
¼ tsp. cayenne pepper
½ tsp. basil
salt and pepper to taste
½ cup chopped green
  onions
filé powder (optional)

Fry the chicken in the oil until brown. Next, fry the andouille for 4 or 5 minutes. Reserve the chicken and sausage. To the oil left in the pot, add the flour and slowly cook to a nice brown.

Place in the pan the onions, bell pepper, and celery and sauté until vegetables are limp. Add the chicken stock, garlic, thyme, bay leaves, cloves, allspice, cayenne, and basil. Carefully add the salt and the black pepper. Let this mixture slowly simmer for at least 40 minutes, then add the chicken and sausage. Cook until the chicken is tender.

Remove from heat and add the green onions. Let it sit for 10 to 15 minutes. Serve over rice. Add a pinch or two of filé powder to each plateful of gumbo if desired. Serves six to eight diners.

When seafood was plentiful and cheap, and the crabs were not fat enough to eat boiled or stuffed, Memere would make SEAFOOD GUMBO.

She had an unerring way of being able to determine whether the crabs were "full" as she said it, or fat. She would grab the crab by its two back flippers with her thumb and forefinger and turn it over and inspect its white belly. If the underside of the crab was bluish or seemed transparent, that crab was not fat, and therefore, good for gumbo. However, if the underbelly was yellow or cream colored, you could bet that it had plenty of meat inside. So with nonfat crabs, a simple seafood gumbo was made—one that didn't require any okra and started with a roux.

Now there are many cooks today who approach the making of a roux with trepidation, and so before we make this gumbo, we're going to discuss a roux. I might point out that there are two ways of making a roux—the slow way and the fast way. Memere and Mamete always made their roux the slow way. They took just about equal amounts of fat (or oil) and flour. Let's take, for example, 4 tablespoons of oil and 4 tablespoons of flour. They put the oil in a heavy pot and then sprinkled a like amount of flour into the oil. They would cook this for a long time—by long I am talking about 30 to 40 minutes on a very low fire, stirring and stirring constantly. You could watch the roux, or the flour, as it changed color from white to cream to golden and finally light brown and then dark brown. This could be stopped at any phase, depending on the color of the roux you desired.

The quick way, or modern way, is to take 4 tablespoons of oil, put it in the pot, and turn the fire very high. When the oil almost reaches the point of smoking, you quickly sprinkle in 4 tablespoons of flour, and with a whisk or slotted spoon, you proceed to stir all the while. In about a minute, the flour begins to change color rapidly. As it begins to get brown, then darker brown, the pot is removed from the fire and the roux stirred until it reaches the deepness of color that you wish. At this point, you add your vegetables—onions, celery, and bell pepper.

Now, before you start your roux for the **SEAFOOD GUMBO,** first boil ½ dozen crabs, 2 pounds of shrimp, and 2 dozen oysters. Reserve the liquid used for boiling as stock. (You need 2 to 2½ quarts of stock or water.) You also need:

¾ **cup oil or lard**	**1 tsp. basil**
¾ **cup flour**	**4 bay leaves**
3 onions, chopped	**½ tsp. chili powder**
1 cup chopped celery	**1 cup chopped shallots**
1 bell pepper, chopped	**¼ cup minced parsley**
4 cloves garlic, minced	**dash Tabasco**
1 6-oz. can tomato paste	**salt and black pepper to**
1 16-oz. can whole	**taste**
tomatoes	**½ stick butter**
½ tsp. thyme	

Using the oil and flour, make a roux as described above. When the flour is a golden brown color, stir in and sauté the vegetables (the onions, celery, and bell pepper), continuing to stir while cooking for 10 minutes. Add the garlic, tomato paste, and whole tomatoes. Cook about 5 minutes, keeping on a low simmer and stirring constantly.

At this point, slowly add the stock or water, mixing as you add. Bring to a simmer and season with the bay leaves, basil, thyme, chili powder, Tabasco, salt, and black pepper.

While the pot is simmering, peel the shrimp and peel and clean the crabs. Combine the butter and about 2 tablespoons oil in a skillet and sauté the shrimp for 2 to 3 minutes. Remove and set aside.

Cut or break the crabs in half, sauté in the same grease for another 5 minutes, and allow to stand in the pan. After the gumbo has cooked for 20 minutes, put the shrimp in and add all the contents of the pan with the crabs. Let this simmer another 20 minutes and add the oysters and their liquid, shallots, and parsley. Cook for 5 minutes, remove from heat, and let stand for 10 minutes.

Serve over hot, fluffy rice. This gumbo can be eaten with a little dash of filé powder. This recipe will serve six or eight people, depending on the size of your servings.

This next seafood gumbo employs the wonderful vegetable, okra. It is said that okra was introduced to the colonies here by African slaves. Fearful of what they would discover in the new world, as the story goes, they smuggled the okra seeds in their woolly hair. When they got to Louisiana, the seeds were planted, and in the fertile soil of Louisiana they flourished. Some have suggested that the Bantu word for "okra" is *kingumbo*. It is evident, if this is true, that there is a strong connection between okra and the soup we call "gumbo."

In selecting okra for a gumbo, always remember to get fresh, tender okra. One way to tell this is to bend the tips of a few of the okra pods before you buy them. If the tips snap off, you know the okra is fresh, but if the tips are soft and pliant and do not pop off, do not use them—they are not fresh.

OKRA SEAFOOD GUMBO

6 hard-shell crabs
2 lbs. okra
2 tbsp. flour
5 tbsp. oil
1 tbsp. butter or margarine
1 cup finely chopped onions
½ cup chopped green
  onions
3 cloves garlic, finely
  chopped
1 green pepper, chopped
½ cup chopped celery

2 lbs. raw shrimp, peeled
  (save heads and shells)
8 cups crab water
1 cup diced, cooked ham
1 11-oz. can tomatoes
1 tsp. salt
¼ tsp. black pepper
5 dashes Tabasco
3 bay leaves
½ tsp. powdered thyme
½ tsp. basil

Boil crabs about 20 minutes in lightly salted water. Remove crabs and reserve the water.

Wash okra and cut into ⅛-inch rounds. Put 2 tablespoons of the oil and the butter or margarine into a skillet (it is best not to use cast iron for cooking okra, as it will discolor the vegetable), and fry the okra until all traces of the sliminess disappear. In a deep pot (again, it is best not to use cast iron) pour the remaining oil and stir in flour to make a roux, cooking until deep brown. Now add onions, garlic, green peppers, and celery. Stir for about 5 minutes and add the ham. Cook for 10 minutes on a low fire and then add tomatoes and shrimp. While this is simmering, take about 8 cups of the salted crab water and boil the shrimp heads and peelings. In the large pot add the okra and stir for a few minutes. Strain the crab/shrimp water and add to the pot. Now add the seasonings and simmer slowly for 2 hours. While the gumbo is boiling, remove the shells from the crabs and clean the crab bodies. Add crabmeat to the pot. Also crack the large crab claws and throw them into the pot. Add green onions during last 5 minutes of cooking. This gumbo should be served over rice. Will serve four to six.

In addition to the seafood gumbos, there are also many other gumbos which the Creoles originated. One of their famous ones was CHICKEN AND SHRIMP GUMBO. Now Memere had a number of chickens in her yard, and every spring when some of the large Rhode Island Reds or Plymouth Rocks went to setting, she would place twenty to twenty-five eggs under one of the hens and would allow her to set on the nest. In twenty-one days we had a new batch of young chickens. These were raised until they were two to three months old and then they were killed and cooked as fryers.

The older hens, of course, were much tougher and did not lend themselves easily to frying or quick cooking. These had to be cooked in a long process such as that required by chicken sausage gumbo or chicken sauce piquante. Anyone who has ever taken the trouble to investigate will usually find that the older chickens have a much better flavor.

When Memere was not using chickens from her own yard, we would get them from the French Market. It was very interesting how she selected the chickens, which were usually bought "on the hoof," so to speak. As we passed the cages where the chickens were kept, Memere would point out a particular chicken and instruct the chicken man to remove it for inspection. The chicken would be taken from the coop and Memere would examine it from its beak to the tip of its feet. She would feel it all over to determine its plumpness or skinniness and would carefully examine the craw (the bag in the neck where food is stored before it is digested) to determine whether there were too many rocks. It's quite possible to have a quarter pound of gravel in a chicken's craw. Now Memere solemnly averred that unscrupulous poultry dealers would feed their chickens small "pea" gravel before they brought them to market, which increased their weight by up to a quarter pound. She was not about to buy a quarter pound of gravel!

One of the important ways she would determine the age of the chicken would be to feel the lower end of the breast bone. If it was flexible, she knew she had a rather young and tender chicken. If it was stiff and unyielding, the chicken was older, meaning that while the meat was a little tougher, it had much more flavor than the younger chicken and lent itself admirably to dishes such as chicken gumbo.

CHICKEN AND SHRIMP GUMBO

1 chicken (or its equivalent
  in parts)
salt and pepper
½ cup oil
6 tbsp. flour
2 large onions, chopped
1 cup chopped celery
1 bell pepper, chopped
4 cloves garlic, minced

2½ qts. water
1½ lbs. shrimp, peeled
Tabasco to taste
½ cup chopped parsley
1 bunch green onions,
  chopped
1 doz. oysters and their
  water
filé powder

If you are using a whole chicken, cut into serving portions. Season the chicken parts with salt and pepper. In a heavy pot heat the oil and fry the chicken until golden brown. Remove chicken from the pot, add flour to the hot oil, and let it cook, stirring constantly until the roux is dark brown. Stir in the onions, celery, and bell peppers and sauté for 5 minutes. Add the garlic and cook for 1 minute longer. Slowly add half the water, simmer, put the chicken back in the pot, and cook slowly until it begins to get tender. Add the shrimp and the rest of the water and let simmer for 15 minutes. Season to taste with salt, pepper, and a few drops of Tabasco. Add the parsley and green onions, cook for 5 more minutes, and add the oysters and oyster water. Cook for 5 more minutes and the gumbo is ready. Serve over hot rice and add a pinch or two of filé powder to each plateful. Will serve six to eight diners.

Ask the next ten Creole cooks you see for their recipe for gumbo and dollars to beignets you'll get ten entirely different recipes (that is, if they'll give you their recipes!). Those gumbos and other Creole recipes were closely guarded family secrets. When I was a child, gumbo was one of our main dishes. It was served at the start of at least half of our meals, and the other half of our meals began with a soup.

The gumbos we ate were divided into three main classifications: those with okra as a base, those with filé added just before serving, and those with neither okra nor filé.

Some Creoles will stoutly maintain that a gumbo must have either okra or filé, and there is a great deal of merit to their position. There are others who just as vehemently uphold the opposing view that a gumbo is a gumbo though it contains neither okra nor filé. This DUCK AND ANDOUILLE GUMBO is a marvelous example of a gumbo with neither okra nor filé.

DUCK AND ANDOUILLE GUMBO

2 mallard ducks, cut into
  serving pieces
1¼ lbs. andouille sausage
2 medium onions, finely
  chopped
1 bell pepper, finely
  chopped
4 stalks celery, finely
  chopped
1 cup cooking oil
1 cup flour
4 cloves garlic, finely
  chopped
3 bay leaves
¼ tsp. allspice

¼ tsp. cayenne pepper
1 tsp. basil
¼ tsp. powdered cloves
½ tsp. poultry seasoning
1 tbsp. salt
6 shakes black pepper
4 tbsp. Worcestershire
  sauce
4 drops Tabasco
5 green onions, finely
  chopped
4 (10½-oz.) cans beef
  consommé
3 cans water

Make a stock with consommé and water in a large, heavy iron pot and bring to a low boil. In a separate heavy iron pot brown duck pieces well in hot cooking oil. (This browning will prevent excess duck fat from cooking out into the gumbo.) When all duck pieces are browned well, place them in the pot of stock. Drain about ¾ cup of the oil and fat from pot used to brown duck and set aside for later use in making roux. Add the chopped onions, pepper, and celery to the remaining hot oil and sauté until very tender, stirring well. When vegetables are cooked, combine them with the duck and stock.

Slice andouille into round slices about ¼ inch thick and brown in the pot used to brown the duck. (Cook out as much grease from the andouille as possible.) Add the browned andouille to the duck, stir well, and maintain cooking at a simmer. As the mixture simmers add the chopped garlic and the rest of the seasonings and stir until all are well blended.

Make a medium dark roux in the pot used for browning duck and sausage. Use the oil and fat saved from browning and an equal amount of flour. When the roux is cooked, remove from heat and add enough stock from the duck and andouille to thin it; then add the thinned roux to the duck and sausage. (If roux is added to duck without thinning it would form lumps.)

Stir mixture well and adjust heat to cook at a low simmer. Cover and cook until duck is very tender (about 2½ hours). At end of cooking remove from heat, add Tabasco, check for salt, add chopped green onions, and let sit for 5 minutes. Serve over rice. Serves six to eight.

The old Creole cooks were almost unanimous in their opinion that the best soup produced in their kitchens was onion soup. I agree—there wasn't anything that we enjoyed more than starting our evening meal with onion soup, complete with toasted French bread and Gruyère, Swiss, or Parmesan cheese.

Mamete, my mother, had her own way of slicing onions that I'll pass on to you. Those of you who slice onions know how difficult it can be sometimes, because as you slice it becomes hard to hold the onion in position. Mamete solved this problem by first cutting the onion in half from the stem end to the root end. Now, the onion could be placed flat on your cutting board and sliced rather easily.

Mamete was a great onion soup maker who always used her own unusual recipe. She would begin by getting the best onions available—the large white ones. Another of her secrets was to use thin slices of slab bacon.

ONION SOUP

8 onions, sliced
6 slices bacon
3 tbsp. flour
4 10½-oz. cans beef
   consommé
2 cans water
1 tsp. basil
¼ tsp. thyme

2 bay leaves
8 to 10 slices French bread
butter
8 to 10 thin slices Gruyère
   or Swiss cheese
grated Parmesan cheese
salt and pepper to taste

Put the bacon in a heavy iron pot and fry at a very low heat. Fry until crisp and remove.

Raise the temperature to medium heat, and sauté the onions in the hot bacon grease. When the onions begin to change color, add the flour and stir continuously, mixing well. Turn the heat down very low and cook for 3 to 4 minutes; do not brown the flour.

Pour in the consommé and water, stirring until the onion, flour, and liquid are thoroughly mixed. (If you can substitute 2 quarts of beef or chicken stock for the consommé and water, it would be even better.) Season the soup with salt and black pepper, but be careful to remember that consommé is already salted. Add the basil, thyme, and bay leaves.

Let this cook for 30 minutes on a slow, simmering fire. While the soup is simmering, toast the French bread slices on one side in your broiler. Butter each slice on the untoasted side and cover each with a slice of cheese. Cut the bacon into 10 pieces and place a piece on each bread and cheese slice. Sprinkle grated Parmesan cheese over all. Put the slices under the broiler until the cheese has thoroughly melted and combined with the bacon.

We are now ready to serve the onion soup. In the bottom of each bowl, place a slice of toast and pour the soup over it. This is soupe à l'oignon at its best.

CRAB SOUP

12 crabs
1 heaping cooking spoon
  flour
¼ lb. butter
1 No. 2 can of tomatoes
2 ribs celery with tops,
  chopped
3 sprigs thyme
1 large onion, minced

4 sprigs parsley, minced
8 slices lemon
1½ tsp. paprika
1 hard-boiled egg, chopped
  fine
6 tbsp. sherry (or 1 tbsp. per
  plate)
salt and pepper to taste

Clean and halve crabs. Melt butter and add flour, mixing constantly until golden brown. Add onions and let simmer for 5 minutes. Add crabs and then pour in 3 cups of hot water. Simmer for 5 minutes.

Mix in tomatoes, celery, thyme, parsley, and 6 cups hot water. Let boil vigorously about ½ hour. Add sherry, lemon, hard-boiled egg, paprika, salt, and pepper. (If soup becomes too thick, pour in water until desired consistency is reached.) Let simmer for ½ hour. Serves six.

GREEN CRAB SOUP

1½ cups split pea soup
3 10¾-oz. cans chicken
  broth
1 lb. crabmeat
½ cup whipping cream

4 tbsp. dry white wine
¼ cup minced shallots
2 hard-cooked eggs, finely
  chopped

In a saucepan, mix the split pea soup and broth and bring to a simmer. After 5 minutes, add the crabmeat and wine and gently stir. Let simmer for 5 minutes and remove from heat. Stir in the cream and serve.

In each bowl sprinkle ½ teaspoon of the chopped shallots on top of the soup and then add 1 teaspoon of the chopped egg. Serves six.

CREAM OF CAULIFLOWER SOUP

1 head of cauliflower
¾ qt. water
1 qt. milk
1 stick butter
10 tbsp. flour

1 bunch green onions
3 tbsp. finely minced
　parsley
salt and pepper to taste

Break up the cauliflower into small pieces and put on to boil in the water. While it is boiling, chop the green onions finely and sauté very slowly in butter over low heat. When the cauliflower is barely tender, remove from heat and add the milk to it.

Combine the flour with the onion and mix well. Cook for about 3 minutes, stirring all the while, and then turn the heat off for a moment. Slowly pour the cauliflower mixture into the flour mixture, stirring continuously until it is well mixed. Now add the salt and black pepper, turn the heat back on, let it come to a simmer (do not boil), and cook for 10 to 15 minutes. Remove from the heat and stir in the chopped parsley. Serve over croutons (optional) to six people.

CREAMED CORN SOUP

3 slices bacon
1 No. 2 can creamed corn
1 large onion, chopped
2 tbsp. butter
2 cups water

1 tbsp. flour
1 qt. milk
2 dashes Tabasco
salt and pepper

Dice bacon and cook over low heat in a heavy soup kettle until almost all the fat has been rendered. Pour off rendered fat and add corn, water, and onion. Cook, stirring often, for 10 to 15 minutes.

In a saucepan, melt butter and stir in the flour; when bubbly add the milk, stirring constantly. Cook, continuing to stir, until steaming hot; then add the corn mixture. Mix well and season to taste with salt, pepper, and Tabasco. Cook and stir for 15 minutes more and it's ready to serve. Makes enough for four.

With the coming of the sunny spring weather, Memere would putter around in the back yard preparing the ground for her herb bed. No experienced Creole cook ever used store-bought herbs and spices in cooking unless it was an ingredient that could not be grown in the surrounding climate or was too difficult to prepare properly (such as filé). Every year we would begin to get ready when the herb-growing season approached.

We had a huge wagon wheel in the yard about five feet in diameter, where we grew our herbs. Pepere had cut about four spokes out of the wheel so that eight compartments were left, in which the different seeds were planted. Of course, parsley was one of the first to be planted; it had an extra long germinating period (almost a month). In the other sections went basil, tarragon, sage, marjoram, dill, rosemary, and a small bird's-eye pepper bush. In a few weeks, along about the beginning of May, some of the seasonings were ready to be cut and used. I haven't mentioned thyme here, because this was grown in another section of the yard. We lived in one side of a double house, each side of which had a long alley that went from the front sidewalk all the way back to the rear of the house. The alley was paved except for a small strip of mud, offering an excellent spot to place thyme. Thyme, as you may know, is a prolific plant and once started, like Tennyson's brook, would grow on and on forever. So we always had a ready supply.

Another pleasant experience about the thyme growing in the alley came about because of the way thyme grows as a ground creeper. As you walked through the alley, your feet were bound to crush some of the thyme, and the wonderful aroma of fresh leaves would assail your nostrils and even come through the windows that bordered the alley. As the thyme needed thinning (it grew like a weed), we'd cut it into pieces about 6 inches long, tie a bunch together with a piece of string, and hang the bunches up to dry. It was with these dry sprigs that Memere would make her bouquet garni, a marvelous seasoning addition to any soup.

CREAM OF POTATO SOUP

BOUQUET GARNI

1 sprig thyme	**2 basil leaves**
2 sprigs parsley	**1 stalk celery**

Split the celery stalk down the long way and separate the two halves. Lay the seasoning in the curved hollow of one piece of the celery and cover with the other piece. Tie the two halves together, leaving enough string to hang the "bouquet" into a soup pot.

2½ cups potatoes, pared and sliced	**½ tsp. onion salt**
1 large onion, chopped	**½ tsp. celery salt**
2½ cups water	**1 cup cream**
½ tsp. salt	**1 tbsp. butter**
2 pinches black pepper	**1 tbsp. finely chopped parsley**

Combine the potatoes, onion, and bouquet garni and boil in water in a large pot. Reduce to a simmer and add the salts and the pepper. Continue cooking until the potatoes are tender.

At this point remove the bouquet garni. Mash the potatoes well in the water in which they were cooked. Stir in the remaining ingredients, simmer, and serve. This soup will be a welcome beginning to the rest of the meal.

CREOLE SOUP

2 cups diced potatoes
2 cups sliced carrots
1 cup sliced onions
salt and black pepper
1 cup light cream or
   evaporated milk
½ cup chopped shallots

1 pinch thyme
2 bay leaves
1 tbsp. finely chopped
   parsley
1 tsp. Tabasco
2½ qts. water

Put the potatoes, carrots, onions, shallots, bay leaves, and thyme in the water. Heat at a simmer until vegetables are very soft. Mash most of the vegetables against the side of the pot and then add the Tabasco and cream; heat gently until "thickish." Season with salt and pepper, sprinkle with the chopped parsley, and serve.

CREOLE VEGETABLE SOUP

5 to 6 lbs. soup meat
2 1-lb. cans tomatoes
4 onions, coarsely chopped
5 carrots, coarsely chopped
5 celery stalks, coarsely
   chopped
⅔ lb. lima beans
1 cob corn per person, cut
   into fourths
½ cup green onions

½ cup parsley
¼ head cabbage, chopped
2 potatoes, quartered
1 tbsp. salt
2 tsp. black pepper
Tabasco to taste
½ tsp. thyme
3 bay leaves
7 qts. water

In a 10-quart stock pot, combine the vegetables, beef, and seasonings. Add the water and bring to a boil. Reduce heat to a simmer, keeping the pot partially covered. Skim off the scum that rises to the top and continue to simmer for about 4 hours. This will make a very thick vegetable soup. Add more water if desired.

If there is any extra stew meat, it will make a meal by itself. Serve with creole mustard or horseradish sauce.

One of the truly admirable traits of Creole cooking, a trait that perhaps we have lost sight of today, was that nothing—I repeat *nothing*—was ever wasted. Never was a crumb of bread or a grain of rice discarded. Any leftovers were sure to find their way into the next day's meal. If it was a surplus of bread the day before, we might have "Lost Bread" or a bread pudding that evening. Or maybe the bread was crushed by Memere's rolling pin into crumbs and used in a gratin or pané dish.

Leftover meats were used in a variety of ways as well, from being served cold on a sandwich, chopped finely and used for stuffing vegetables, served in a glacé, or in some of the most delectable hashes. Hashes were not considered second class fare in our house, because when Memere or Mamete turned out their hash onto a serving platter, it was Creole cooking at its best.

One of the best hashes was made from soup meat from the previous day. The vegetable soup was always seasoned with soup bone and brisket. Enough brisket was always cooked so that some would be left over. The brisket was always added when the soup had been simmering for some time. This sealed the juices in and added to the flavor of the meat. When the meat was almost tender, potatoes were added to the pot. When the potatoes were tender, the meal was ready. First, a plate of soup was served. Then the meat was removed from the liquid, along with the potatoes, and became the entrée.

The next day we had hash. The meat was chopped into fine pieces and the boiled potatoes were cubed. To a skillet was added a spoonful of lard and a finely chopped large onion, ½ cup chopped celery, and a chopped bell pepper. The vegetables were sautéed until very tender, then the meat and potatoes were added, along with some salt and black pepper. Over a moderate to almost high heat, the hash was cooked until the potatoes were beginning to brown. Then ½ cup finely chopped green onions and 2 cloves of minced garlic were stirred in. When the hash was brown it was ready. Heavenly **HASH**!

The ingredients again are:

leftover soup meat, finely
  chopped
boiled potatoes, cubed
1 tbsp. lard
1 large onion, finely
  chopped
½ cup chopped celery

1 bell pepper, chopped
salt to taste
¼ tsp. black pepper
½ cup finely chopped green
  onions
2 cloves garlic, minced

One of the marvelous ways Mamete would fix leftover rice was in **RICE SOUP.** For this she used:

4 tbsp. butter
1 large onion, chopped
2 cups chopped green
  onions
2 cloves garlic, minced
2 tbsp. minced parsley
4 tbsp. flour
1½ qts. chicken or beef
  stock

1 cup cooked rice
2 cups shredded lettuce
1 small can petit pois,
  drained
salt and pepper
a couple good dashes of
  pepper sauce

Melt the butter in a large saucepan. Add the onion, and cook over low heat until tender. While the onion is cooking, add about ¼ teaspoon black pepper. Add the green onions and garlic, and sauté about 2 minutes. Stir in the parsley. When well mixed, sprinkle in the flour. Cook the flour, stirring constantly, for 3 to 4 minutes. Slowly add the stock, stirring until smooth. Bring the soup to a simmer and let cook for 10 minutes. Add the rice, lettuce, salt and pepper to taste, pepper sauce, and peas. Simmer, allowing to cook no longer than 3 minutes. Serves six to eight.

OYSTER ARTICHOKE SOUP

2 doz. oysters and their
   water
2 bunches shallots,
   chopped
½ lb. butter
5 tbsp. flour

1 14-oz. can artichoke
   hearts
2 bay leaves
salt
white pepper

Poach the oysters in their own water. Strain, reserving water, and set aside.

Sauté the shallots in melted butter. When the onions are transparent add the flour. Mix well, stirring constantly, for 5 minutes. Add oyster water and the juice from the artichoke hearts. Pour in additional water to make enough for eight to ten diners. Add 2 bay leaves, and salt and white pepper to taste. Slowly bring to a boil. Chop the oysters and artichoke hearts and add to the soup. Cook for a few more minutes and serve.

PARSLEY CREAM SOUP

½ stick butter
2 onions, sliced
2 celery ribs, cut into thin
   slices
4 potatoes, peeled and
   diced

5 cups chicken stock
1½ cups chopped parsley
salt and pepper to taste
2 cups light cream

Melt the butter in a large saucepan. Add the onions and celery, and sauté over a low heat until vegetables are tender. Add the potatoes and chicken stock and mix well. Cook at a slow simmer until potatoes are soft. Add the parsley and simmer for 3 or 4 more minutes. Remove the soup from heat and let cool slightly. Puree in a blender and season with salt and pepper.

This can be served either warm or chilled. Just before serving, stir in the cream. Serves six to eight diners.

SHRIMP AND CORN SOUP

5 tbsp. oil
3 tbsp. flour
2 onions, finely chopped
1 bell pepper, chopped
4 shallots, chopped
2 tbsp. minced parsley
2 lbs. shrimp, peeled and
  coarsely chopped
salt and pepper to taste

⅛ tsp. cayenne pepper
2 dashes Tabasco
1 can (1 lb. size) tomatoes,
  undrained
1 can (1 lb. size) whole
  kernel corn, undrained
3 cups chicken stock (more
  may be added if a thinner
  soup is desired)

Make a roux with the oil and flour. When golden brown add the onions. Sauté slowly for 10 minutes, and then add the bell pepper, shallots, shrimp, parsley, salt, pepper, cayenne, and Tabasco. Simmer 5 more minutes, then add the tomatoes, corn, and stock. Simmer for 1 hour.

Serves six to eight.

SPLIT PEA SOUP

1 1-lb. pkg. dry split peas
1 ham bone or 1 cup
  chopped ham
3 qts. chicken or beef stock
  (water may be
  substituted)
4 stalks celery, finely
  chopped
2 medium onions, chopped

2 carrots, scraped and
  chopped
salt to taste
½ tsp. black pepper
1 tbsp. Worcestershire
  sauce
2 tbsp. finely chopped
  parsley

Put all ingredients except the parsley in a large pot. Bring to a boil and then reduce heat. Simmer slowly for 2 hours. If you are using a ham bone, remove it and chop the meat into small pieces. Return ham to pot. Cook for ½ hour longer, then serve.

Sprinkle a pinch of chopped parsley over soup in each plate. Serves six to eight.

GREEN ONION AND POTATO SOUP

2 bunches green onions, chopped	3 tbsp. flour
4 medium-sized potatoes, peeled and diced	2 qts. water
	cream (1 tbsp. per each plate)
3 tbsp. butter or margarine	salt and pepper to taste

Sauté the green onions in the butter for 5 minutes. Add the flour and stir, mixing well. Slowly pour in the water; bring the mixture to a boil. Add the potatoes, salt, and pepper. Cook until the potatoes are tender (about 20 to 25 minutes).

When ready to serve, put about 1 tablespoon of cream in the bottom of each plate and pour the soup over it. Serves six to eight.

The other day, as I strolled through the "new" French Market, I couldn't help but feel a bit of sadness for what had been done in the area in the name of progress and remodeling.

It was beautifully, and, I guess tastefully, rebuilt—and of course some of the buildings of the old market were certainly in need of repair—but as I observed the gift shops, restaurants, and other tenants, I got the overall sense that something old had been destroyed just because it was old. It seemed to me almost like chrome plating an old piece of fine pewterware to renew it.

As I meandered along, nostalgia began to rear its sentimental head, and I hearkened back to the twenties, when the conglomeration of buildings was the hub of a confused cacophony of the most delightful sounds, sights, and smells. I began to reminisce about my tri-weekly visits with Memere, who with her shopping basket on her arm, went through the vegetable, poultry, and meat sections, and finally went on to the seafood places where the most interesting and intriguing sights and smells were to be found.

There we found mounds of freshly caught fish, including redfish, red snapper, catfish, trout, flounder, and pompano. The bins or wire boxes of crabs and crawfish were the next interest-getters. I would stare in amazement as the men in their rubber boots and aprons, with absolutely no fear of the snapping claws, would reach in barehanded to handle the crabs and crawfish. Also, there would always be large mounds of fresh turtle meat. I would stand spellbound, watching the meat move and twitch, even after it had been cut from the turtle. Tradition had it that it would not stop moving until the sun went down. But long before sundown, Memere usually had a couple of pounds of the meat well on the way to becoming a delicious TURTLE SOUP.

The first thing she did was melt ¾ cup butter in a heavy soup pot. Then she would gradually add about 8 tablespoons of flour, stirring constantly. This would be cooked over low heat until the roux was a nice medium-brown color. Memere then added ½ pound of chopped lean ham, 1 cup of chopped onion, 3 coarsely chopped medium-sized tomatoes, ¼ cup chopped celery tops, 1 chopped bell pepper, and 4 toes of garlic, finely chopped. She thoroughly mixed it all together and cooked the mixture over a low heat until the vegetables browned (about ½ hour).

Then 2 pounds of turtle meat were chopped into small pieces and added, together with 2 teaspoons salt, ⅔ teaspoon black pepper, 2 pinches cayenne pepper, 4 bay leaves, ½ teaspoon powdered thyme, ¼ teaspoon cloves, ¼ teaspoon allspice, ¼ teaspoon grated nutmeg, 4 cups beef stock or 3 cans beef consommé, and 1½ cups water. All of this was brought to a boil, and then lowered to a simmer and cooked for 2½ hours.

About ½ hour before the soup was done, 1 teaspoon Worcestershire, 2 thin slices of lemon, and 4 tablespoons of sherry were added. Ten minutes before it was finished, ⅛ cup finely chopped parsley was added. (If the soup needed thinning, a little water was added, too.) When everything was done, the soup was allowed to "set" for 15 minutes in the pot so the seasonings would blend. What a soup this made!

Just before serving, you could add 2 sliced hard-cooked eggs. Dig down deep when serving the soup to get the solids at the bottom. Have a big slice of crisp French bread ready to eat with the soup, too. Serves four to six.

TURTLE SOUP

¾ cup butter
8 tbsp. flour
½ lb. lean ham, chopped
  into small pieces
1 cup chopped onion
3 medium-sized tomatoes,
  coarsely chopped
¼ cup chopped celery tops
1 bell pepper, finely
  chopped
4 garlic toes, finely
  chopped
2 lbs. turtle meat, chopped
  into small pieces
2 tsp. salt
⅔ tsp. black pepper

2 pinches cayenne pepper
4 bay leaves
½ tsp. powdered thyme
¼ tsp. cloves
¼ tsp. allspice
¼ tsp. grated nutmeg
4 cups beef stock (or 3 cans
  beef consommé)
1½ cups water
1 tsp. Worcestershire
2 thin slices lemon
4 tbsp. sherry
⅛ cup finely chopped
  parsley
2 hard-cooked eggs, sliced

VICHYSOISSE

6 leeks, thinly sliced
6 green onions, thinly
  sliced
2½ lbs. potatoes, peeled
  and thinly sliced
1½ sticks butter

1½ cups half-and-half
1 cup milk
2 tbsp. chopped chives
salt and pepper to taste

Melt the butter in a deep pan. Sauté the leeks and green onions over low heat until they are soft. Add the potatoes and enough water to cover them. Bring to a boil, then reduce the heat and let simmer for 1 hour. Remove from the heat and press through a sieve. Refrigerate for at least 1 hour.

Just before serving, stir in cold milk and half-and-half. Add the salt and pepper, and when well mixed, sprinkle the chives over the soup. Serve cold to six to eight diners.

There was no doubt that we had the whitest box steps in the neighborhood! This was a matter of pride and prestige and, being always the perfectionist, Memere was never satisfied with anything less than the best. On our street all the houses had box steps which descended from the front door right on to the banquette or sidewalk. There were usually four steps leading up to the front door. On either side of the steps was a boxlike affair, the top of which was as high as the top step, even with the doorway of the house. Those were the days before any kind of air conditioning or even window fans, so the family would find refuge sitting on the box steps in the cool breeze of the evening. To stir the air a little, the women of the family would sit with their palmetto fans trying to manufacture a little breeze.

The steps were cleaned every day, weather permitting. As I grew to the point where I could carry a bucket of water, the scrubbing of the front steps became one of my regular chores. I would go out to the front to scrub the steps early in the morning. My equipment consisted of a bucket of water, a scrub brush, a box of Grandma powder, and a small bucket of red brick dust. (I digress for a moment to explain the brick dust. Whenever we could, we would collect the old, soft, red clay bricks. We would break them into smaller pieces and rub the pieces together. In a short time the pieces would disintegrate into a fine red powder. This would be used as an abrasive to scour the wooden steps.) The steps were wetted down first, then sprinkled with Grandma powder (the popular soap powder of the day). The steps were scrubbed with the brush, rinsed, and then the brick dust was spread over the wood. A little more scouring was needed and then the steps were rinsed with clean water. Somehow, the Grandma powder and the brick dust seemed to develop a powerful bleaching action because when the steps dried, they were a gleaming white.

Then I would hurry away from my chores and into the kitchen to watch Memere fix her delicious **SPLIT PEA SOUP.**

First, she would need a hambone, so whenever the grocer had one available, you can be sure Memere would swoop it up. Along with the hambone she would use:

3 tbsp. bacon drippings (If
   not available, use 3 tbsp.
   lard or cooking oil.)
2 large onions, finely
   chopped
4 cloves garlic, minced
1 carrot, finely chopped
2 bay leaves
½ tsp. sage
1 pkg. (1 lb.) dried split
   peas
½ cup chopped, cooked
   ham

2½ qts. beef stock (If no
   stock is available, use
   water and 8 beef bouillon
   cubes.)
½ lb. fresh mushrooms
½ cup finely chopped green
   onions
½ tsp. sugar
4 dashes Tabasco
salt and black pepper to
   taste

Put the bacon drippings into your soup pot and sauté the onions, garlic, carrot, bay leaves, and sage over a medium fire. Cook until the onions are soft. Add the peas, soupstock, ham, and hambone and bring to a boil. Reduce the heat until the mixture simmers, and cook for 2 hours.

While the pot is simmering, slice the mushrooms and sauté them in butter for a few minutes. About 15 minutes before the soup is finished cooking, add the mushrooms, sugar, Tabasco, salt, pepper, and green onions. Simmer for 15 minutes more, then serve with pieces of crisp French bread. Serves six to eight.

CREAM OF MUSHROOM SOUP

1 lb. mushrooms
1 stick butter
1 qt. milk
1½ qts. chicken stock
1 onion
salt and pepper
1 bunch green onions, finely
   chopped

8 tbsp. flour
2 bay leaves
1 tsp. basil
½ tsp. Tabasco
4 or 5 chicken bouillon
   cubes

Boil the onion, bay leaves, basil, and tops of the green onions in the stock for ½ hour. (The stock can be homemade or canned chicken stock.) Strengthen the stock with 4 or 5 chicken bouillon cubes. Strain.

In a heavy pot, melt the butter over a low heat; add the flour. Cook for 5 minutes, stirring constantly. Add the milk very slowly. When the sauce is well mixed and creamy, slowly pour in the strained stock.

Clean the mushrooms, remove the stems, and chop finely; add to the soup. While this cooks, slice the mushroom tops. After the soup has simmered for about 10 minutes, add the salt and pepper to taste, the Tabasco, and the sliced mushrooms. Let cook for another 5 minutes, stirring occasionally. When the soup is served, garnish each bowl with about a teaspoonful of chopped green onions. Serves eight to ten.

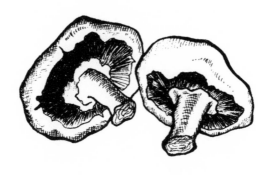

salads

Ask any Creole cook where you can learn to make the world's finest salad and he will promptly offer to teach you. Memere and Mamete were no exceptions; they were good salad makers. Memere had certain rituals and rules about making good salads from which she never varied.

First, she insisted on the freshest greens possible. This rule is almost impossible not to violate today, with the limp, insipid greens offered by today's grocery stores. I think about the only way one can enjoy the taste of fresh, crisp greens today is by getting them directly from the truck farms. Try going sometimes to the vegetable section of the French Market. There are times when you can get wonderful salad material.

Let's start off with a **LETTUCE SALAD**, always one of my favorites. Try to find some fresh bibb lettuce, the loose leaved, wonderfully green variety. If you can, shun completely the tasteless, white, tight, iceberg heads.

Rule number two: do not cut the lettuce. Disassemble or break up into leafy pieces carefully with your hands. After this is done, add water to the bowl and swish around gently. Drain and wash again, then drain and remove as much of the water as possible from the greens. There is a gadget nowadays that spins the greens dry by turning a crank. Memere sometimes dried the greens by dumping them on a towel.

The first thing the Creole cooks did after the greens were dried was to mix in a "chapon," a piece of dried French bread rubbed all over with a freshly cut clove of garlic. Some who wanted a little stronger garlic taste rubbed the interior of the salad bowl with a cut clove of garlic, or for a still stronger taste, mashed a whole clove of garlic into a paste in the bottom of the bowl.

Okay, toss the chapon into the greens. Next, take about 1 tablespoon oil, pour over the greens, and mix thoroughly until each piece of lettuce is coated. This preserves both the flavor and the crispness.

Add vinegar and more oil. Whether the vinegar is wine, cider, or distilled is your preference. (I prefer apple cider vinegar.) The best ratio to use is three to one in favor of the oil. Toss until the salad is thoroughly mixed. At this point, you can add sparkle by mixing in 3 tablespoons finely chopped shallots and 1 tablespoon chopped parsley.

The last thing to add is the salt and pepper. Incidentally, if the salad is prepared well in advance, do not salt until you are ready to serve. After tossing thoroughly, the chapon is always removed.

Of course, the salad combinations are endless and are limited only by your own imagination. Another delightful salad combines slices of onion, cucumber, and tomato.

One last tip: you have heard it said that you shouldn't wash a salad bowl. That's hogwash! If the bowl is wood, the oil will sooner or later sink in and become rancid, and will give a bad taste to your salad. A glass or plastic bowl is about the best you can use.

Let me pass along to you Memere's recipe for a **SPINACH SALAD** that's "out of this world"! First, get about a pound of fresh spinach. (If you can get the packaged greens, you'll save yourself a lot of washing time.) Pick the spinach for discolored leaves and remove the stems. Put the leaves in a colander and wash well. Set aside to drain.

Fry 6 strips of bacon until crisp and then chop very finely. Drain the bacon grease from the pan and put in 4 tablespoons of olive oil, 2 tablespoons salad oil, a couple of shakes of Tabasco, and 4 minced green onions. Let the onions sauté over a very low heat for 5 minutes.

While the onions sauté, slice ½ pound of fresh mushrooms. Add the mushrooms to the pan along with 1 tablespoon Creole mustard. After mixing well, allow to cook about 3 minutes longer over a very low heat.

Now we're ready to put the salad together. First, be sure the spinach is dry. Take the oil, mushrooms, and the rest of the mixture from the pan and pour over the spinach. Drop in your chapon, along with 2 pinches of salt, and mix.

Toss until the greens are well coated with oil. Remove the chapon, sprinkle with the chopped bacon, 1 chopped hard-cooked egg, and ¼ cup grated Parmesan cheese, and mix well. Now you're ready for a truly great salad!

Another salad that was a favorite of mine was made with okra, tomatoes, and onion. Mamete took ½ pound of fresh okra and boiled until tender. (She always added a spoonful or so of lemon juice to the water, claiming it reduced the slipperiness.) When the okra was ready it was drained, the tough stem ends were cut off, and it was then put into the salad bowl. To the okra were added 2 white onions, thinly sliced. Over this was poured a vinaigrette dressing. (Vinaigrette dressing is a mixture of 4 tablespoons olive oil, 1½ tablespoons apple cider vinegar, a drop of hot pepper sauce, and ½ teaspoon Creole mustard.) The salad was gently mixed and then 2 tomatoes which had been cut into eighths were added. Mamete mixed a little more, added salt and pepper to taste, and then the salad was ready.

I might add here that a good rule to follow for any salad dressing is to be lavish with the oil and stingy with the vinegar. Actually a three to one ratio will make a good vinaigrette dressing. Again, always be sure the greens are dry. These two simple rules, if followed, will make a better salad.

ONION SALAD

2 onions, sliced into rings
1 or 2 green onions,
  chopped
3 tbsp. oil

1 tbsp. vinegar
salt and pepper to taste

Mix together in a bowl the onions and green onions. Add the oil, vinegar, and salt and pepper to taste. Toss thoroughly.

This makes a good topping for steamed cabbage or red beans and rice.

CREOLE POTATO SALAD

5 lbs. potatoes
1 large onion, finely
  chopped
4 ribs celery, finely chopped
6 scallions (green onions),
  finely chopped
6 hard-cooked eggs, finely
  chopped
2 tbsp. minced parsley
2 beef bouillon cubes

2 tbsp. dry white wine
5 tbsp. olive oil
2 tbsp. wine vinegar
2 tbsp. lemon juice
4 drops Tabasco
1 pinch powdered thyme
salt and black pepper to
  taste
1 cup mayonnaise

Boil the potatoes until soft; drain and cool until they can be handled easily. Peel and cut into slices about ¼ inch thick. Place in a bowl, pour in the olive oil, wine vinegar, and lemon juice, and mix well. Add the onion, celery, scallions, parsley, and eggs and mix gently. Add the wine, Tabasco, thyme, and salt and pepper to taste.

Put the bouillon cubes in about 2 tablespoons water and allow to slowly boil until the cubes are dissolved. Pour over the salad.

MAYONNAISE

2 egg yolks
salt and pepper to taste
¼ tsp. dry mustard

¾ cup oil
2 tbsp. lemon juice

NOTE: All of the ingredients for the mayonnaise should be at room temperature.

Beat the egg yolks and the seasonings in a bowl with a whisk or an electric mixer until thick. Add the oil drop by drop, beating all the while. When about 2 tablespoons of the oil have been added, the mixture should be very thick. At this point, stir in 1 tablespoon of the lemon juice. The remaining oil can now be added at about a tablespoon at a time; beat well. When all the oil has been added, add the remaining lemon juice and salt and pepper to taste. Pour over the potato salad and mix well. Serves ten to twelve.

CREOLE RICE SALAD

3 cups cooked rice
4 hard-cooked eggs,
  chopped
1 cup crisp fried bacon,
  crumbled
½ cup chopped sour pickles

2 tbsp. olive oil
½ cup chopped celery
½ cup chopped onions
½ cup chopped shallots
½ cup mayonnaise
1 tbsp. vinegar

Mix all ingredients and chill before serving. This will serve about ten to twelve.

Memere had a saying that went something like this: "May lightning strike very soon the cook who measures herbs by tablespoons." I guess this was said in disdain of anyone who was so unsure of oneself as to have to measure the herbs and spices as one cooked, and who seasoned too heavily. She never measured any seasoning that went into any dish she cooked, and boy, how she knew her seasoning! Many of the more popular herbs she grew in her garden.

Many of the herbs were also used for medicinal and other purposes. She said basil, for instance, would develop a cheerful and merry heart. There was also an old-time custom avowing that if a woman in labor held in her hand a sprig of basil and the feather of a mockingbird, her baby would be born without any pain.

Of course, aside from its magic qualities, basil also contributed zest and flavor to a variety of different foods. A few fresh leaves, finely chopped, would do wonders for salad dressings. Also, basil was great when added to stews and egg dishes, and of course in any tomato dish. The old Creoles also believed that a basil plant inside kept the flies out of the room.

Incidentally, if you are using fresh instead of dried herbs, always remember to use twice as much fresh as dried. Strange, is it not? You would think just the opposite would be true.

Another wonderful seasoning that Memere grew in pots in her kitchen and back porch was chives. She always maintained that chives were a good remedy for bleeding. Chives are one of the easiest herbs to grow and extremely rich in sulphur, which is continuously needed in the human system. Chives can also be used just any time you would like a mild onion flavor in cooking. They are especially delectable on jellied or chilled soups, particularly vichyssoise.

The dill plant, Memere would tell me, would protect the individual in the area where it was grown from evil spirits and witches. I don't know how true this was, but Memere had a pot of dill in her yard and I never saw an evil spirit or witch at any time! There was also an old custom that burning the dried dill plant drove away thunder clouds and cleared the air. Early American settlers used to call dill seeds "meeting house seeds" because they were carried to church and munched on when the service was too long. Brides used to put a sprig of dill in their shoes along with a dash of salt for good luck and a happy marriage. On the practical side, dill makes a wonderful seasoning for salads, fish, meats, and soups and of course, is used everywhere in pickling cucumbers.

But let's get back to basil, just about my favorite herb. Here's a recipe for salad dressing that I think you'll like. It costs about one-third as much as the commercially prepared kind.

Take 4 tablespoons apple cider vinegar, 1 teaspoon garlic salt, 1 teaspoon finely cut basil leaves, and salt and pepper to taste. Mix all these together in a jar and shake vigorously. Now add ¾ cup of a half-and-half mixture of olive oil and vegetable oil and shake again.

This can be used over any salad. Also, it's a good dressing to baste with if you're broiling beef or liver.

VINAIGRETTE DRESSING

¼ tsp. salt
¼ tsp. black pepper
1 tsp. Dijon mustard
1 tbsp. finely chopped
  shallots

1 tsp. finely chopped
  parsley
3 tbsp. vinegar
8 tbsp. olive oil
1 tsp. lemon juice

Combine all the ingredients in a bowl except the lemon juice and olive oil; mix well. Now add the olive oil in a thin stream. When well mixed, add the lemon juice.

This dressing can be refrigerated. Shake well before using. For a garlic dressing, proceed as above, adding 3 smashed and finely chopped garlic cloves in the first step.

CREAM FRENCH DRESSING

¼ tsp. salt
¼ tsp. black pepper
1 tsp. Dijon mustard
1 tbsp. finely chopped
  shallots

1 tsp. finely chopped
  parsley
3 tbsp. vinegar
⅓ cup heavy cream
1 tsp. lemon juice

Combine all of the ingredients except the lemon juice and cream; mix well. Slowly add the cream and lemon juice, mixing thoroughly. Shake well before using.

LEMON EGG FRENCH DRESSING

1 hard-cooked egg yolk
4 tbsp. oil

2 tbsp. lemon juice
salt and pepper to taste

Mix all of the ingredients to a creamy consistency.

HERB FRENCH DRESSING

2½ tbsp. chopped mixed herbs (You may use fresh anise leaves, tarragon, parsley, basil, marjoram, chives, thyme, and/or mint.)

double the ingredients of VINAIGRETTE DRESSING (See recipe.)

Prepare in the same manner as the VINAIGRETTE DRESSING. (See my recipe.) Add the mixture of herbs and mix well.

ROQUEFORT DRESSING

¼ lb. mashed Roquefort cheese
¼ tsp. salt
1 tsp. Dijon mustard
1 tbsp. finely chopped shallots
1 tsp. finely chopped parsley

3 tbsp. vinegar
7 tbsp. olive oil
1 tsp. lemon juice
2 tbsp. heavy cream
2 drops Tabasco
¼ tsp. black pepper

In a bowl, blend the salt, pepper, mustard, shallots, parsley, and vinegar together. Add the olive oil in a thin stream, whisking constantly. Blend in the lemon juice, Roquefort cheese, cream and Tabasco. Correct the seasonings if necessary.

Before we leave the "salad bar," I've got to include two classic Creole salads that I've enjoyed over the years, Memere's CRAWFISH SALAD and Mamete's CABBAGE SALAD.

For the **CRAWFISH SALAD** you'll need:

2½ **cups boiled crawfish**
   tails, chopped rather
   coarsely
5 **ribs celery, finely chopped**
   (Try to use the inner,
   more tender ribs.)
6 **shallots, finely chopped**
2 **hard-cooked eggs,**
   chopped

1 **dill pickle, finely chopped**
1 **tbsp. Worcestershire**
   sauce
1 **cup mayonnaise (Why not**
   make it yourself?)
salt and pepper to taste

Combine all the above ingredients except the mayonnaise, salt, and pepper, mixing thoroughly. Mix in the mayonnaise, and then the salt and pepper. If you are using crawfish that have been boiled in a "courtbouillon," be sure to season carefully.

This will serve four to six.

Now for the **CREOLE CABBAGE SALAD.** Mind you, this is *not* a slaw, because it contains no mayonnaise.

You'll need:

1 large head of cabbage	1 tsp. dried basil
½ cup olive oil	¼ tsp. powdered thyme
2 beef bouillon cubes	4 cloves garlic, minced
1 onion, very finely chopped	3 tbsp. wine vinegar
1 bunch shallots, finely chopped	4 or 5 drops hot pepper sauce
2 tbsp. minced parsley	salt and pepper to taste

First, shred the cabbage as finely as you can. This can be done with a sharp chef's knife. Wash the cabbage and drain well. Be sure the cabbage is dry. (This is important.) Put the cabbage in a salad bowl and pour over it half of the olive oil. Now mix and mix until all the cabbage is coated with the oil.

Put the 2 bouillon cubes with 2 tablespoons of water in a very small pan and heat until the cubes are dissolved. Allow to cool, then pour over the cabbage. Add the onions, shallots, parsley, basil, thyme, and garlic and mix very well. Add the rest of the olive oil, the vinegar, and pepper sauce and toss until well mixed. Add the salt and pepper to taste.

This will serve six to eight. I believe it's one of the truly great salads in the Creole culinary repertoire!

*sauces &
seasonings*

I've heard it said many times that one of the basic differences between French cuisine and Creole cooking was that the French used innumerable sauces in their dishes and the Creoles did not. This, dear reader, is certainly not the case. It is true that French cooking relied on sauces for their succulence, and through their culinary history, French ingenuity accounted for hundreds of different sauces, but so did the Creoles!

A story epitomizing the Frenchmen's search for perfection concerns a certain French chef who boiled down and reduced 50 hams to 1 cupful of liquid which was used as a basis for a sauce he was inventing. Imagine 50 hams!

But the truth about the Creole use of sauces is the fact that they are simplifications of some of the most complicated of the French sauces. It is interesting to note, for example, the recipe for bechamel sauce in the New Orleans *Times-Picayune Creole Cook Book*. You need ham, mushrooms, butter, veloute sauce, cream, celery, carrots, onions, herbs, cloves, allspice, and even a blade of mace! Now, BECHAMEL SAUCE, as we know it today and as these Creole cooks modified it, is a simple white sauce. First, 2 tablespoons of butter are melted in a heavy saucepan. Two tablespoons of flour are added slowly and the mixture stirred constantly. When the flour is thoroughly blended, ¾ cup of milk is added, stirred in, and allowed to cook slowly. Then 2 drops of Tabasco, ¼ teaspoon freshly ground nutmeg, and ½ teaspoon of salt are added. That's bechamel as we know it today.

To make a good MORNAY SAUCE, all that is necessary is about ½ cup of shredded cheese added to the bechamel and cooked slowly until the cheese is melted. This sauce is very good on such diverse foods as cabbage, cauliflower, or spaghetti.

BORDELAISE is another sauce that has evolved into a rather simple undertaking. It is made with butter, olive oil, and garlic. First, melt ½ stick of butter in a saucepan; add 2 tablespoons olive oil and let warm 2 or 3 minutes. Add 5 or 6 coarsely chopped cloves of garlic, ½ teaspoon salt, and ¼ teaspoon black pepper. Cook this over high heat for 4 to 5 minutes. As the garlic begins to brown, quickly remove it from the sauce with a slotted spoon. Turn off the heat and add 1 tablespoon finely minced parsley. Try this sauce on spaghetti, or dip pieces of broiled shrimp or lobster in it.

Another excellent sauce to have in your repertoire is HOLLAN-DAISE. Put 3 egg yolks in a 2-quart saucepan. In a separate small pan, melt 1 stick of butter. When it is melted, remove it from the heat. Put the pan with the egg yolks on a very, very low heat and beat with a wire whisk. After 2 or 3 minutes, it should begin to thicken. At this point, add about ⅓ of the melted butter, continuing to heat until mixed. Remove the saucepan from the burner and slowly add the rest of the butter, beating all the while. After this is mixed, put the pan back on the burner and add 1 tablespoon lemon juice and a pinch of cayenne pepper. Stir slowly, and there it is—SAUCE HOLLANDAISE! Try this on broccoli. It's delicious!

BECHAMEL SAUCE

2 tbsp. butter
2 tbsp. flour
¾ cup milk
2 drops Tabasco

¼ tsp. freshly ground
   nutmeg
½ tsp. salt

MORNAY SAUCE

2 tbsp. butter
2 tbsp. flour
¾ cup milk
2 drops Tabasco
½ tsp. salt

¼ tsp. freshly ground
   nutmeg
½ cup shredded Gruyère or
   Swiss cheese

BORDELAISE SAUCE

½ stick butter
2 tbsp. olive oil
5 or 6 cloves garlic,
   coarsely chopped

½ tsp. salt
¼ tsp. black pepper
1 tbsp. finely minced
   parsley

HOLLANDAISE SAUCE

3 egg yolks
1 stick butter

1 tbsp. lemon juice
pinch of cayenne pepper

BEARNAISE SAUCE

1½ cups dry vermouth
2 shallots, minced
6 peppercorns
½ tsp. dried tarragon
1 bay leaf

¼ tsp. powdered thyme
2 egg yolks
1 stick butter
1 tsp. minced parsley
white pepper to taste

Place the vermouth, herbs, and seasonings into a glass or enamel saucepan. Boil until reduced to 1 tablespoon. Put the egg yolks in a bowl; strain the vermouth and add to the egg yolks. Place over a pan of gently simmering water (or use a double boiler). Whisk the yolks with a wire whisk until they are slightly thickened. Add the butter, small pieces at a time, whisking all the while. (Slip the butter through your fingers as you add it. This will soften the butter.) Cook until the sauce is thick and creamy. Stir in the parsley, season with the white pepper, and it's ready to serve.

AVOCADO DIP

1 ripe avocado, cut into
   small pieces
1 8-oz. pkg. Philadelphia
   cream cheese
3 tbsp. cream

2 tbsp. lemon juice
¼ small onion, finely
   chopped
2 shallots, finely chopped
¼ teaspoon salt

After the cream cheese has been softened at room temperature, mash in and cream the avocado. When thoroughly mixed, add the rest of the ingredients. (This can also be done in a blender.) To add a colorful touch, a little green food coloring can be added.

MAYONNAISE

1½ cups oil
1 large egg yolk
2 tsp. mustard
1 pinch freshly ground
  pepper

a few dashes vinegar
  (preferably wine vinegar)
water
salt to taste

Place the egg yolk in a bowl, add mustard, pepper, and salt to taste, and blend together. (Use fork or whisk.) Add the oil, drop by drop, while beating steadily. (Do not try to pour the oil too quickly.) If the mixture becomes too thick at the beginning, dilute with a few drops of water. When you have enough mayonnaise, add some water and vinegar to taste. This will make the mayonnaise smoother. Also, by adding water to the vinegar, the mayonnaise will not curdle.

Remember these four points:

1. *It takes 1 big egg yolk for less than 2 cups of mayonnaise.*
2. *The oil should be at room temperature.*
3. *At the beginning, the oil must fall drop by drop on the mustard and egg blend.*
4. *Take care that the egg, vinegar, or lemon juice and water are at the same room temperature.*

CREOLE TARTAR SAUCE

3 egg yolks
1½ cups olive oil
1 tbsp. Creole mustard
¼ tsp. cayenne pepper
1½ tsp. salt
½ cup finely chopped
   shallots

½ cup finely chopped
   parsley
½ cup finely chopped dill
   pickles

With a whisk, beat the egg yolks vigorously in a deep bowl for about 2 minutes until they thicken. Start to add the oil _very slowly_, beating all the while, until the sauce is thickened. Add the mustard, cayenne, and salt, and beat until the sauce is smooth. Stir in the chopped shallots, parsley, and pickles and taste for seasoning. The sauce is ready to be served or can be refrigerated 2 or 3 days before serving.

REMOULADE SAUCE

¾ cup olive or salad oil
¼ cup lemon juice
¼ cup Creole mustard or
   prepared brown mustard
2 tbsp. prepared
   horseradish
⅔ cup finely chopped onion
⅔ cup finely chopped celery
2 tbsp. finely sliced green
   onions with tops

2 tbsp. finely chopped
   parsley
2 tsp. paprika
1 tsp. salt
⅛ tsp. pepper
⅛ tsp. cayenne
1 clove garlic, minced

Combine all of the ingredients and mix well. Chill. Makes approximately 2½ cups.

Serve over seafood or with sliced meats. May be stored, covered, in refrigerator 4 days.

Keep seasonings on your shelf only until they begin to lose their strength. For most, this means no longer than 3 months. You can test the strength of your seasoning by crushing or rubbing a bit in the palm of your hand, letting it warm slightly, and then sniffing it. Keep herbs and spices tightly covered and away from the light as much as possible.

It's a good idea to cook with one herb or spice at a time until you learn its characteristics. A good way to try new herbs and spices is in an omelet. When using herbs in soups, stews, gumbos, and sauces, it is a good idea to add during the last hour of cooking. Fresh and dried herbs can be used interchangeably, but, if a recipe calls for dried herbs and you use the fresh, you must use two to three times as much.

The important seasonings are bay leaf, basil, thyme, and black pepper.

BAY LEAF

This seasoning from the laurel tree has been called the foundation flavor for Creole cuisine. It should be used sparingly because it is a strong seasoning. It is used in cooking meat, fish, and poultry. One or two leaves are enough in a soup or stew for serving six people. The leaves should be removed before serving.

BASIL

Many good cooks consider basil the finest on the herb shelf, and it is one of the herbs most easily grown. It is wonderful with tomatoes, seafood, meats, poultry, and potatoes. When chopped fine and mixed with butter, it makes a delightful spread.

THYME

This is another indispensable ingredient in Creole cooking. It is mainly used in stuffings, soups, meat, and fish dishes and with a great many vegetables. It can also be easily grown.

BLACK PEPPER

Black pepper can be bought as whole peppercorns or ground. The freshly ground pepper is more flavorful than the other. White pepper is the same as the black. They are both from the same peppercorn. The white is peeled first, before being ground. White pepper is used in white sauces, where the black specks might be objectionable.

CAYENNE

Cayenne is another useful flavor, but be careful using it because it is very hot. Dried red peppers can also be used. (Boil the dried peppers for a couple of hours in a small amount of water and add the liquid by the teaspoon until the desired hotness is reached.)

ALLSPICE

Allspice is used in fruit pies, cakes, spice cake, mince meat, plum puddings, and other desserts. It can also be used in gumbos, stews, and gravies. It should be used sparingly—⅛ teaspoon or less per dish.

CLOVES

It is almost impossible to count the ways cloves can be used in Creole cooking. Cloves are used in sweet as well as savory dishes, but like allspice should be used sparingly—⅛ teaspoon or less.

POULTRY SEASONING

Poultry seasoning is a very good, all-purpose seasoning that can be used for many dishes in addition to poultry. It is a mixture of most of the important seasonings, including sage, oregano, ginger, rosemary, marjoram, thyme, celery seed, and pepper. It adds an excellent flavor to shrimp and crawfish etouffée.

CHILI POWDER

This seasoning is a blend of chili powder, red pepper, oregano, cumin, and garlic powder. Chili powder is a very good flavor to add to any tomato sauce, although it is also good in soups, stews, and gumbos. You can get two kinds, the mild and the hot.

CURRY

Some curries contain as many as a dozen ingredients, including turmeric, cardamon, coriander, mustard, fennel, mace, allspice, and various peppers.

BOUQUET GARNI

Bouquet garni consists of parsley, thyme, and bay leaf tied together. It is mostly used in soups, gumbos, and stews.

FINES HERBES

Parsley, chervil, chives, and tarragon fall into this category. Memere would make her fines herbes by wrapping a small piece of cheesecloth around 2 or 3 bay leaves, a sprig of thyme, a couple of fresh basil leaves, and sometimes a clove or two. The cloth was tied with a piece of string and lowered into whatever she wanted to season. She left the string long enough to drape over the side of the pot so that she could remove the seasoning by pulling the string.

GARLIC

Garlic is universally used, and is one of the favorite seasonings in Chinese and Creole cooking. Do not use a garlic press, because the results will usually be bitter. Also, do not allow the garlic to burn when sautéeing. If burned, the dish will become bitter.

FILÉ

Filé was given to the Creoles by the Choctaw Indians. The Indians used it as a medicinal herb. Filé induces perspiration. In French, filé means to "make threads," and thus it should not be cooked. When soup or gumbo is served, add the filé to the plate. This is the proper way to use this seasoning.

Of course, there are many other good seasonings to learn about, such as marjoram, oregano, rosemary, savory, tarragon oil, ginger, and others.

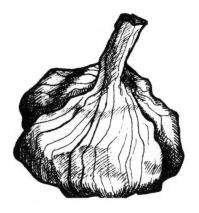

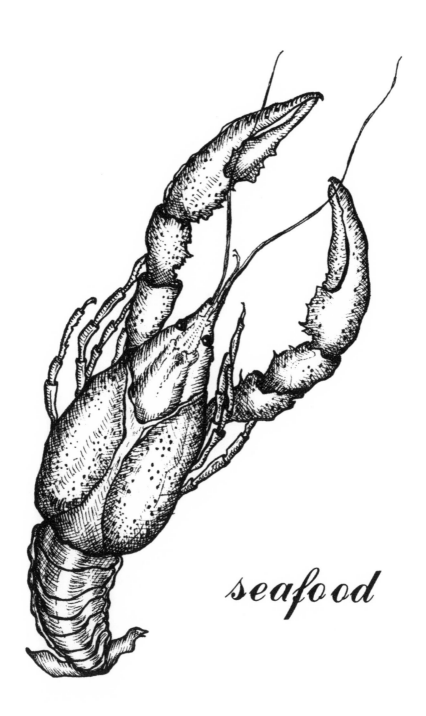

seafood

Very often I am asked, "If you had to eat just one dish for the rest of your life, which one would you choose?" On impulse my answer is CRAWFISH BISQUE. And after I have committed myself to the bisque, I can always justify my selection with encomiums of praise about that delectable Creole creation.

Gradually a bit of nostalgia begins to intrude, and then after due reflection, BISQUE ECREVISSE becomes my number two selection, while the winner becomes Mamete's BOUILLABAISSE, a dish the Creoles borrowed from the French. The Creoles made so many marvelous improvements that the Marseilles version stands only as a weak imitation of "Bouillabaisse à la Nouvelle Orléans." Of course, I confess here and now that I have never been to Marseilles and have never partaken of the true, or "Le Vrai" bouillabaisse, as the Marseillais like to call this seafood soup. And, of course, they point out that without rascasse, boudion, vive, salinette, and other fish indigenous to their area, any other bouillabaisse has to be considered counterfeit. But not so, dear reader, and I quote no less an authority than the great writer and gourmet, William Makepeace Thackeray, who referred to New Orleans as the "Old Franco Spanish city on the banks of the Mississippi, where, of all the cities of the world, you can eat the most and suffer the least, where the claret is as good as in Bordeaux, and where a ragout and a bouillabaisse can be had the like of which was never eaten in Marseilles or Paris." Bravo, Mr. Thackeray, and allow me to add a few words to explain why Creole bouillabaisse is second to none in the world! Where, except in New Orleans, could you have handy, red snapper, redfish, trout, crawfish tails, shrimp, oysters, crabmeat, and soft shell crab to put in the pot for your bouillabaisse?

But the proof of the bouillabaisse is in the eating, and to eat it you have to prepare it. The recipe that follows is not an easy one. It's complicated and requires a great deal of time and patience, but I have no doubt that if you try it, you'll feel as I do that it is truly a masterpiece from a Creole kitchen.

CREOLE BOUILLABAISSE

1 qt. fish stock
½ stick butter (unsalted preferably)
6 tbsp. olive oil
2 large white onions, finely chopped
1 or 2 carrots, chopped
2 bay leaves
1 bunch green onions, finely chopped
3 ribs celery, finely chopped
3 cloves garlic, minced
1 tbsp. minced parsley
2 tbsp. flour
4 whole ripe tomatoes, peeled and roughly chopped
3 cups chicken broth
1 lb. shrimp, peeled, cleaned, and deveined
2 doz. raw oysters
1 cup oyster water

1 lb. crabmeat (claw)
1 lb. peeled crawfish tails
4 small soft shell crabs, salted, peppered, and browned in 2 tbsp. butter and 2 tbsp. oil, then cut in half crosswise
1½ tsp. salt
1 tsp. cayenne pepper
½ tsp. black pepper
1 tsp. powdered thyme
¼ tsp. ground allspice
¼ tsp. ground cloves
1 tsp. chili powder
4 lbs. filleted fish (at least 2 kinds, preferably 3, such as red snapper, redfish, trout, or drums, cut into 3-in. pieces)
½ cup dry white wine
a pinch or two of saffron

First, make a fish stock with the bones and heads of the fish you have filleted. Put the fish in 2 quarts of water, along with the bay leaves, the green tops of the green onions, and a chopped carrot or two. Let this boil slowly for 20 minutes and your stock is made.

In a large, heavy pot melt the butter, add the olive oil, and sauté the onions, green onions, celery, garlic, and parsley over low heat for 6 to 8 minutes. Stir in the flour and cook 5 minutes longer. Add the tomatoes, salt, cayenne and black pepper, thyme, allspice, cloves, chili powder, 1 quart of strained fish stock, and the chicken broth. Bring this to a rolling boil and then lower the heat to a simmer. Cook for 25 minutes.

Meanwhile, rub the fillets with salt and black pepper and bake in a

350-degree oven for 15 minutes. After 25 minutes, add the shrimp, oysters and their water, crawfish, crabmeat, and fried soft shell crabs to the pot. Allow to cook for 5 minutes, then add the wine and saffron. Add the baked fillets and cook for 5 more minutes, correcting the seasoning.

To serve, place a slice of toasted French bread in the bottom of each bowl, place one-half of a soft shell crab on top, and fill the bowl with the soup. Garnish with lemon slices. Serves ten to twelve.

Along about springtime, Pepere, my grandfather, used to look up at the sky and say, "I'll bet the crabs are getting fat out at Lake Pontchartrain." This was a sure sign that on the following weekend we would be off to the lake. We would leave on Saturday or Sunday morning, with our baskets, nets, sacks, sandwiches, and, of course, a number of hand lines, together with a cast net that Pepere was very proud of, having knitted it himself. We would walk over just a couple of blocks from the house where "Smoky Mary," an actual train, ran along Elysian Fields straight out to the Lake, or to old "Millenberg" (Milneburg).

Once out at Milneburg, the first thing we did was bait our crab nets. We used the various parts of chickens—the backs, necks, and sometimes the wings—that Memere had saved during the week. Having baited the nets, we threw them into the water. Then I would take off my shoes and root around in the sand and in the very low water for clams. It did not take long to collect a bucket of these clams, which we promptly smashed with a brick or a little hammer Pepere had brought for that purpose. Then we "baited" our area of the Lake. We took the smashed clam shells, brought them out to a little deeper water, and threw them in. Once on the bottom, these smashed clams attracted a lot of the shrimp we were after. We had tried to eat the plentiful supply of clams, but unfortunately they were full of the muddy sand or the sandy mud that constituted the bottom of the lake.

Then Pepere, after a few minutes, would cast his net out into the water to pull in the shrimp. It wasn't long until we had a few dozen crabs and a few pounds of shrimp, together with a dozen or so croakers and occasionally a speckled trout. Then we would eat our lunch, and by that time it was time for Smoky Mary to come back. Incidentally, the fare amounted to 15 cents, and I have heard it said that this was one of the oldest railroad lines in the United States.

Once home, Memere did wonderful things with the seafood we brought back. First, she boiled the crabs, and then divided them into a few piles—one for stuffed crabs, one for gumbo, and, if we had enough, one for just sitting at the table and eating. She would usually put the shrimp on ice (we had iceboxes in those days) to cook the next day.

When we had eaten our fill of the boiled crabs, Memere would then begin to pick the crabmeat. After she had picked about a pound of crabmeat, she carefully wrapped it and again put it on top of the ice, with the idea that the next day we would eat STUFFED CRABS for our dinner.

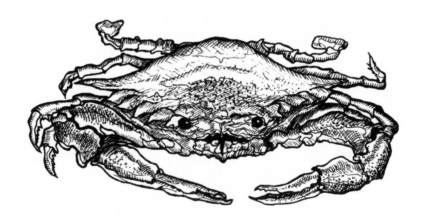

STUFFED CRABS

2 cups crabmeat
1 onion, minced
4 stalks shallots, minced
½ cup seasoned bread
  crumbs
1 tbsp. minced parsley
1 stick butter
juice of 1 lemon
½ cup light cream

1 tbsp. sherry
2 hard-cooked eggs,
  minced
salt and black pepper to
  taste
⅛ tsp. cayenne
⅛ tsp. powdered thyme
8 crab shells

In ½ stick of butter, sauté, over a very low fire, the onions and shallots. When the vegetables are soft add the bread crumbs and mix well. Now add the crabmeat, parsley, eggs, cream, and sherry, and mix together lightly so as to break up the pieces of crabmeat as little as possible. Sprinkle in the salt, black pepper, cayenne, and thyme. Stir a little and let sit off the fire a few minutes.

Take the crab shells (be sure they are clean and smooth inside) and lightly rub with butter on the inside. Fill the shells with the stuffing. When the shells are filled, sprinkle very lightly with seasoned bread crumbs, dot with a small piece of butter, and spoon the lemon juice over each stuffed crab. Bake in a 375-degree oven a few minutes until the top starts to brown slightly.

What concerned most of the families in our neighborhood in my youth were three main interests. The first, of course, was the church. Everybody in our area was Catholic. This meant that all of the different feast days, fast days, and days of abstinence, as well as many other different customs, were observed. We carried palms to church on Palm Sunday, made our Easter duties, ate our gumbo z'herbes on Holy Thursday, and had ashes put on our forehead each Ash Wednesday. Always, as St. Joseph Day approached, there were at least half a dozen altars on our block alone and so religion played its part in our daily lives.

Next came family, with grandfather and grandmother, mother, father, and the children usually making up the household, with some families even having great grandparents in their midst. There was no question where our duty lay. "Honor thy father and thy mother" was a well-kept commandment in our neighborhood.

The third influence? Well, would you believe the daily activity involved consorting with the lottery vendors who plied their trade in the area? It would begin at 10:00 A.M., after the men in the family had gone to work. Around the corner of Frenchmen and Urquhart, a rather nondescript character would wend his way. He would walk up to the front steps and conduct his business through the blinds. The blinds would always be drawn tightly, and when the communication had been established, the shutters would be opened and a small bit of paper, wrapped around a couple of coins, changed hands. This was Memere's "bet" for the day.

Her gambling would amount to fifty to seventy-five cents per week, and involved an intricate system of numbers, numbers that represented every activity of her life. If there was a birthday or anniversary you could be sure those numbers were played that day. For example, my birthday was March 3. On my birthday Memere would write the numbers 3-13. (She added one to the second three and my age, three numbers altogether.) Then came the waiting. During the day, if any two housewives came together, you could bet the lottery numbers played that day would be the subject of their conversation.

At about three o'clock in the afternoon, the lottery lists were delivered, and you learned the good or bad news, whether your numbers had won or lost. But win or lose, the daily routine of the household continued. For the evening meal, with maybe some crabs left over from the previous day's dinner, Memere would fix a **CRAB BISQUE.**

For this delicious bisque you will need:

1 stick butter
4 large, fat boiled crabs
1 medium to large onion,
  finely chopped
2 ribs celery, finely chopped
4 shallots, finely chopped
4 tbsp. flour
2 qts. chicken stock or 6
  cans undiluted chicken
  broth

2 bay leaves
¼ tsp. powdered thyme
1 pt. half-and-half or light
  cream
salt and pepper to taste
½ lb. white or lump
  crabmeat

First, clean the crabs and cut each one in half. Melt the butter in a heavy pot and sauté over a very low heat the onion, celery, and shallots. (Do not brown.) When the vegetables are tender, add the crab and sauté for about 5 minutes. Sprinkle in the flour and blend into a roux. Cook and stir for another 5 minutes.

Add the chicken stock or broth, the bay leaves, and thyme and simmer 45 minutes. Heat the cream and stir into the soup. Add the salt and pepper, and, if you like, strain the sauce.

Add the crabmeat and serve with crisp French bread. Serves eight.

CRAB PATTIES

1 lb. fresh lump crabmeat
5 green onions, finely
   chopped
4 celery stalks, finely
   chopped
1 cup bread crumbs
1 10½-oz. can beef
   consommé
2 hard-cooked eggs, finely
   chopped
1 tbsp. cornstarch
½ stick butter

3 tbsp. cooking oil
¼ tsp. ground nutmeg or
   mace (Mace is the outer
   shell of nutmeg.)
¼ tsp. thyme
pinch of allspice
pinch of cloves
2 drops of Tabasco
salt
black pepper
flour

Sauté the onions and celery in hot cooking oil in a heavy iron pot until well cooked and soft. As these sauté, add the nutmeg, thyme, allspice, cloves, Tabasco, salt, and black pepper, stirring constantly. Moisten the cup of bread crumbs with part of the consommé (to the consistency of a pie crust) and add to the seasoned vegetables. Mix well. Lower the heat, add crabmeat, chopped eggs, and cornstarch, and stir well.

Remove the mixture from the pot and make into crab patties approximately 1½ inches in diameter and ¾ inches thick. Coat each patty well with flour. Heat the butter and the cooking oil in a heavy iron pot and fry each crab patty until well browned and crisp. Set patties aside when fried.

CRABMEAT MORNAY

1 stick butter
2 tbsp. flour
6 green onions, chopped
1 tbsp. minced parsley
1 pt. breakfast cream or
  half-and-half

½ lb. grated Swiss cheese
2 tbsp. dry white wine
1 lb. lump crabmeat
salt, pepper, and cayenne to
  taste

Sauté green onions and parsley in the butter until the onions are limp. (Do not brown.) Add flour. Blend together and begin adding cream gradually until the sauce is smooth. Add cheese, wine, and seasonings.

Fold in the crabmeat very gently so as not to break up the lumps. Simmer for a minute or two. Serve immediately.

At a very early age I began to absorb my family's attitude toward food, cooking, and eating. Memere and Mamete, for example, were two housewives who really loved to cook. The preparation of food for them was no chore, but rather a delight. They enjoyed their kitchens and it was a source of pleasure for them to watch their families sit down to a meal prepared by them.

I also remember their attitude about the food they served at the table. It was one of reverence, one of dining after having given thanks to the "Grand Provider" for the daily meal. After thanks had been given, Pepere (my grandfather), or Papete (my father) would take the loaf of bread (always a long French loaf), turn it over, and with a knife cut a cross into the crust. Then the bread was sliced or broken and distributed. With this kind of "dinner table" prologue, it was natural that a sort of awe and reverence about food developed.

But it went even further. We all knew that food should never be wasted. To waste food was a sin! Whatever was put before us was eaten. This idea has become so ingrained in my character that even today I cannot bear to see food wasted. Whenever and wherever I eat, I always clean my plate. "As the twig is bent, so the tree is inclined." Another rule about eating that always prevailed was that no one came to the table angry, excited, or perturbed in any way. Being over-wrought or disturbed was considered harmful to the digestion, and so you would wait, calm down, and then come to the table. Memere always said, "Celui qui boude, mange de boudin," which meant "He who sulks, eats his own stomach." It was a favorite saying of her mother, my great grandmother. Mind you this was long before the days of psychosomatic medicine, and yet those old Creoles knew that for good digestion, you had to approach the dinner table in a happy frame of mind. In that happy frame of mind we would often sit down to Memere's Creole CRAB STEW. We usually had some boiled or stuffed crabs the evening before, and having six or eight boiled crabs and some crabmeat left over, it had to be used.

CRAB STEW

½ doz. boiled crabs
4 tbsp. lard or oil
2 large onions, finely
  chopped
4 toes of garlic, minced
2 ribs celery, finely chopped
1 bell pepper, finely
  chopped
4 tbsp. flour
3 cups beef stock or water
1 lb. crabmeat

a couple of pinches of
  powdered thyme
3 bay leaves
¼ tsp. chili powder
1 tbsp. minced parsley
½ cup finely chopped green
  onions
1 tbsp. Worcestershire
  sauce
salt and black pepper to
  taste

First, open the crabs, discard the shells, remove the apron, claws, and gills (or dead men), and cut each body in half. Melt the lard or heat the oil over a low fire. Add the onions, garlic, celery, and bell pepper and let fry slowly until brown, about 10 minutes. Mix in the flour and cook, stirring until brown. Slowly stir in the stock or water and then add the crabs, crabmeat, thyme, bay leaves, and chili powder. Slowly simmer for 30 minutes. Add the parsley, green onions, Worcestershire sauce, and salt and pepper. Stir well, cook for 5 more minutes, and then remove from the heat. Let stand for 5 minutes.

Serve the crab stew over a mound of fluffy, white rice. Serves six to eight.

CRAB PUFFS

WHITE SAUCE

1 tbsp. butter
1 tbsp. flour

½ cup milk
salt and pepper to taste

Melt the butter in a small saucepan. Add the flour and let cook for a couple of minutes over low heat, stirring constantly. Slowly pour in the milk and let the mixture come to a simmer. Add the salt and pepper and let the sauce cook until it thickens.

2 tbsp. minced celery
½ cup minced onion
1 tbsp. green onion
1 tbsp. oil
½ lb. crabmeat
½ cup thick white sauce

2 eggs, well beaten
⅛ tsp. black pepper
½ tsp. garlic salt
½ cup cracker crumbs
1 tbsp. minced parsley

Sauté the celery, onions, and green onions in the oil. Drain the vegetables on a paper towel, then combine with the crabmeat, white sauce, eggs, seasonings, cracker crumbs, and parsley.

Shape into balls, and drop by teaspoonsful into hot oil. Deep fry until golden brown. Drain and serve with tartar sauce.

CRABMEAT DIP

1 8-oz. pkg. Philadelphia
  cream cheese
1 stick butter
1 lb. white crabmeat
1 small white onion, finely
  chopped

3 shallots, finely chopped
dash of Tabasco
2 cloves garlic, very finely
  chopped
a pinch of cayenne pepper
salt and pepper to taste

Melt the butter and cream cheese over a very low heat. Mix in the crabmeat and the rest of the ingredients and keep warm.

This can be served as a dip or in the small patty shells.

Along about June, M'sieu "Le Mud Bug" was just about ready to bid us goodbye for the season, fold his claws, and silently swim away. But before he left, we would gracefully move into summer with the euphoric feeling of having polished off a bowl or two of wonderful Creole **CRAWFISH ETOUFFÉE.** First, we had to get our "crawfish picking" hands on about 10 pounds of live crawfish.

Mamete, my mother, used to say that June crawfish were the hardest to peel and the most delicious to eat. It seemed that about this time of year, the shells got much thicker, making them more difficult to crack, but the crawfish were more mature and more full flavored. The more formidable the obstacle, the greater the reward.

To make this delicious etouffée, first you need 10 pounds of crawfish to boil. (If you don't want to start from scratch, you can begin with 1 pound of crawfish tails.) Wash the live crawfish well a couple of times, then leave them for about 15 minutes in salted water to "purge." Even before you start this, though, have the courtbouillon in which the crawfish will boil cooking on the stove. Put about 3 gallons of water in a pot and add to this 1 chopped onion, a few ribs of celery, 4 bay leaves, 1 chopped lemon, 1 teaspoon black pepper, ½ teaspoon cayenne or Tabasco, and ½ cup salt. Let this boil while you clean the crawfish.

When the crawfish are ready, dump them into the pot. Bring to a boil again, and cook for no longer than 10 minutes before you remove the crawfish. Cool the crawfish and peel. Set aside 1 cup of the courtbouillon for later. (If you decided to buy the crawfish tails from your friendly seafood dealer, ask him for about 1 pint of the water in which he made his crawfish "boils.")

To assemble the etouffée, first you need the crawfish, and also:

¼ lb. butter
2 onions, chopped
2 ribs celery, chopped
3 toes garlic, minced
1 bell pepper, chopped
2 tbsp. flour
1 tbsp. tomato paste
¼ tsp. thyme
½ tsp. basil

¼ tsp. ground cloves
¼ tsp. chili powder
1 tbsp. lemon juice
½ cup crawfish water
½ cup water
½ cup chopped green
   onions
2 tbsp. minced parsley
salt and pepper to taste

First, melt the butter in a large, heavy skillet. Add the onions, celery, garlic, and bell pepper and sauté over low heat for about 20 minutes, or until the vegetables are very soft. Add the crawfish tails, tomato paste, thyme, basil, cloves, chili powder, lemon juice, crawfish water, and water. Mix well and cook for about 15 minutes. Add salt and pepper to taste. Cover and let simmer for another 10 minutes. Add the green onions and parsley.

Remove from the heat and let stand for about 10 minutes, covered, to allow the seasonings to blend. All you need now is some rice to serve it over and a hunk of crisp French bread.

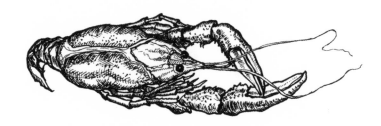

CRAWFISH ETOUFFÉE

3 tbsp. margarine
1 cup finely chopped onions
½ cup finely chopped celery
½ cup finely chopped green
  pepper
3 tbsp. flour
2 tbsp. tomato paste
½ tsp. poultry seasoning
1½ cups crawfish tails (Also
  add fat from the heads.)

2 cups stock
½ cup finely chopped
  shallots
2 tbsp. finely chopped
  parsley
1 tsp. salt
¼ tsp. black pepper
⅛ tsp. cayenne pepper

STOCK:

3 or 4 cups water
crawfish claws and heads

tops of green onions

First, make the stock by boiling the crawfish heads and claws in the water. Add the tops of the green onions and boil for 15 to 20 minutes.

Sauté the onions, celery, and green pepper in the margarine. Cook slowly, stirring constantly, until the vegetables are limp or well done. Stir in the flour, and cook for 10 minutes. Add the tomato paste and cook 10 minutes longer. Add poultry seasoning, crawfish tails, and fat from the crawfish heads. Cook for 5 minutes, and then stir in the stock.

Simmer for 15 minutes, then add the shallots, parsley, salt, black pepper, and cayenne pepper. Simmer for 10 minutes longer, and then allow to "set" for 20 minutes off the fire.

Reheat and serve over rice. (You can also use this recipe for shrimp etouffée.)

CRAWFISH BISQUE

Season 3 gallons of water with 1 package of crawfish boil, to which has been added a couple of chopped onions, 1 sliced lemon, ⅓ box of salt, a couple of cloves of garlic, and 2 tablespoons of black pepper. Allow to boil for about 20 minutes before adding 10 pounds of live crawfish. Let boil slowly for 20 minutes.

After the crawfish have cooled, peel the tails, remove the fat from the heads, and pick out about 30 of the largest heads. Crush the rest of the peeling, heads, and claws, and boil in about 3 quarts of water for ½ hour. After this has cooled, allow it to settle. Strain and reserve for later. This will serve as stock.

Prepare the stuffing for the heads by combining 2 tablespoons of finely chopped parsley, ½ cup finely chopped onion, 4 chopped green onions, 2 finely chopped cloves of garlic, and 2 cups chopped crawfish meat. Fry all of this together in 5 tablespoons butter. Add 2 slices of bread that have been soaked in milk, 1 egg, and the crawfish fat. Add salt and pepper to taste. Use this mixture to stuff the heads, packing tightly. Dip each in flour and fry in hot fat until brown.

Make a roux with 5 tablespoons oil, 5 tablespoons flour, 1 large onion, chopped, one bell pepper, chopped, and 1 cup chopped celery. When the flour is brown and onions are limp, add 1 14-ounce can of tomato sauce, 3 ounces of tomato paste, and 3 finely chopped cloves of garlic. Stir for about 15 minutes and add the stock to reach the desired thickness. Add 3 or 4 bay leaves, 1 teaspoon basil, ½ teaspoon thyme, and 5 to 10 drops (depending on taste) of Tabasco.

Drop the heads and the remainder of the crawfish into the mixture, along with 3 slices of lemon and salt and pepper to taste. Simmer slowly for 1 hour. Serve over boiled rice.

STOCK:

3 gals. water
1 pkg. crawfish boil
2 or 3 onions, chopped
1 lemon, sliced

⅓ box salt
2 or 3 cloves garlic
2 tbsp. black pepper
10 lbs. live crawfish

STUFFING:

2 tbsp. finely chopped
   parsley
½ cup finely chopped onion
4 green onions, chopped
2 cloves garlic, finely
   chopped
2 cups chopped crawfish
   meat

5 tbsp. butter
2 slices bread
milk
1 egg
crawfish fat
salt and pepper to taste
flour
cooking oil

ROUX:

5 tbsp. oil
5 tbsp. flour
1 large onion, chopped

1 bell pepper, chopped
1 cup chopped celery

ADD TO ROUX:

1 14-oz. can tomato sauce
½ 6-oz. can tomato paste
3 cloves garlic, finely
   chopped
3 or 4 bay leaves
1 tsp. basil

½ tsp. thyme
5 or 10 drops Tabasco (to
   taste)
salt and pepper to taste
3 slices lemon

CRAWFISH CARDINALE

1 lb. crawfish tails, cleaned
  and peeled
1 stick butter
3 tbsp. flour
½ tsp. salt
½ tsp. white pepper
1 bunch shallots

3 cloves garlic, minced
3 tbsp. chopped parsley
½ cup white wine
2 tbsp. tomato paste
milk (enough to make a
  medium cream sauce)

Melt ½ stick of the butter in a heavy saucepan. Add the flour, mix well, and slowly add milk until you achieve the thickness of a medium cream sauce. Set aside.

In a skillet slowly sauté the shallots and crawfish until the onions are soft. Add the garlic, white pepper, salt, and parsley and let simmer for a couple of minutes. Combine the mixture with the cream sauce and stir constantly while adding the wine and tomato paste. Let this slowly simmer for 3 or 4 minutes, then turn the heat off. Let set for 2 or 3 minutes, and then serve over mounds of fluffy rice. Serves four.

SHRIMP CREOLE

3 lbs. peeled shrimp
4 tbsp. butter
1 tbsp. oil
6 tbsp. flour
1 14- to 16-oz. can tomato
  sauce
1 cup finely chopped onions
3 ribs celery, chopped
½ cup finely chopped bell
  pepper
3 cloves garlic, minced

½ tsp. thyme
3 bay leaves
1 tsp. chili powder
¼ tsp. cayenne pepper
¼ tsp. black pepper
salt to taste
6 shallots, finely chopped
2 tbsp. minced parsley
3 cups of hot water
1 tsp. sugar
2 thin lemon slices

Sauté the shrimp in a large skillet in the butter and oil for 6 minutes. Remove the shrimp from the pan and add the flour. (Be sure the heat is low.) Stir the flour and butter mixture until lightly browned, then add the onions, bell peppers, and celery. Sauté until the vegetables are tender, stirring all the while.

Add the tomato sauce, water, thyme, bay leaves, chili powder, sugar, garlic, salt, lemon slices, and black and cayenne pepper. Stir well, then cover the pot and simmer for 15 minutes. Add shallots, shrimp, and parsley and let set on back of the stove for 10 minutes.

Serve over hot rice. Serves four to six.

SHRIMP AMANDINE

3 lbs. shrimp
½ cup olive oil
3 tbsp. vegetable oil
½ cup lemon juice
6 tbsp. butter
2 cloves garlic, finely
   chopped

1 cup slivered almonds
2 dashes Tabasco
4 tbsp. dry white wine (such
   as Chablis or vermouth)
½ cup finely chopped
   shallots
¼ tsp. salt

Peel the shrimp and marinate in olive oil, vegetable oil, lemon juice, and garlic about 2 hours. Remove the shrimp and reserve sauce.

Melt the butter and sauté the shrimp and shallots until shrimp are pink (about 6 minutes). Remove shrimp and shallots, and place them on a warm platter. Add almonds, salt, and reserved marinade to the butter in the skillet. Add Tabasco and wine and let simmer for 3 to 4 minutes. Pour over shrimp in platter.

Serve over rice. Serves six.

It seems as though I remember (How often do we look back in time and imagine we experienced certain events?), Memere telling me about a certain gourmet who fervently wished that his neck was as long as a crane's or a swan's, so that the enjoyment of swallowing his food could be prolonged. In later years, I discovered that this thought had been expressed by the Greek gourmet, Philoxemus.

Memere's thoughts about Mr. Philoxemus were always followed by her observation that he was wrong—if he wished to enjoy the prolongation of culinary pleasure, he should have desired a nose like Cyrano de Bergerac, so that the odors of cooking could have been enjoyed more through a heightened sense of smell than taste.

I've thought about this through the years and, by gosh, I think Memere was on the right track. I do believe that food, most of the time, can be enjoyed more and certainly longer through the sense of smell rather than taste.

Memere would often astonish me with her references to literary characters, since I knew for certain that she had no better than a few years in grammar school.She would also astound me with her knowledge of grand opera, but she had a good explanation for this. Pepere (her husband, my grandfather) had a great love for the stage.

Now in those days, stage entertainment consisted of operatic performances at the old French Opera House, located at that time on Toulouse Street. Pepere always managed to find himself a part in the opera—as part of the mob scene, or maybe changing scenery. His pay for his duties was a couple of free tickets, and so for years, Memere was able to attend hundreds of performances. As a result, she developed her own operatic repertoire. As a small boy, I remember her entertaining me night after night, as she sang the aria from the operas.

But I have digressed. To really prove for yourself the pleasures involved in inhaling the odors of food cooking, try this.

Melt 3 tablespoons each of butter and cooking oil in your heavy pot. Add 6 tablespoons of flour, stirring over low heat, until the flour is browned. (You are making a roux.) If you have done it right, it takes at least 20 minutes of cooking. Dump in the pot 2 cups of chopped onions, 1 cup of chopped bell pepper, 1 cup of chopped celery, and 4 toes of chopped garlic.

Stir and smell! Inhale those great odors. Since you have started your dish, add 1 6-ounce can of tomato paste and mix well. Add 2 10½-ounce cans of beef consommé and 2 cups of water. While this slowly simmers, add 3 bay leaves, 1 teaspoon basil, ½ teaspoon thyme, 1 teaspoon chili powder, ¼ teaspoon cayenne pepper, ¼ teaspoon black pepper, and 1 teaspoon salt. After the mixture has simmered 45 minutes, add 3 pounds of peeled shrimp, 1 cup chopped shallots and 2 tablespoons chopped parsley.

Let this cook for about 20 minutes until the shrimp are done. Let the pot stand on the back of the stove for another hour to let the seasonings blend. Reheat if necessary and serve over rice.

This is **SHRIMP ETOUFFÉE** at its best!

ROUX:

3 tbsp. butter
3 tbsp. cooking oil
6 tbsp. flour
2 cups chopped onions
1 cup chopped bell pepper
1 cup chopped celery
4 toes garlic, chopped
1 6-oz. can tomato paste
2 10½-oz. cans beef
   consommé
2 cups water

3 bay leaves
1 tsp. basil
½ tsp. thyme
1 tsp. chili powder
¼ tsp. cayenne pepper
¼ tsp. black pepper
1 tsp. salt
3 lbs. peeled shrimp
1 cup chopped shallots
2 tbsp. chopped parsley

BARBECUE SHRIMP

7 to 8 lbs. large shrimp
2 sticks butter
1 cup olive oil
½ cup chili sauce
¼ cup Worcestershire
2 lemons, thinly sliced
4 cloves garlic, minced
4 tbsp. lemon juice

1 tbsp. minced parsley
2 tsp. paprika
2 tsp. oregano
3 tsp. red cayenne pepper
1 tsp. Tabasco
2 tbsp. liquid smoke
salt and pepper to taste

Wash the shrimp well and spread out in a shallow pan. Combine all of the ingredients above in a saucepan over low heat. Let simmer for 10 minutes, then pour over the shrimp. Mix well and refrigerate for 2 to 3 hours. Baste and turn the shrimp every 30 minutes.

Preheat the oven to 300° and bake the shrimp for 30 minutes, turning them at least every 10 minutes.

This can be served in a soup bowl with chunks of French bread to sop up the sauce.

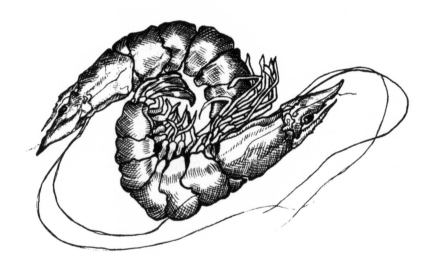

SHRIMP JAMBALAYA

3 lbs. shrimp
1 lb. smoked sausage
2 tbsp. oil
1 tbsp. butter
1 cup chopped onions
1 cup chopped green
　peppers
½ cup finely chopped celery
1 16-oz. can tomatoes
3 cloves garlic, chopped
¼ cup chopped fresh
　parsley

2 cups beef stock or water
½ cup chopped green
　onions
2 bay leaves
1 tsp. thyme
1 tsp. basil
⅛ tsp. cayenne pepper
1 tsp. salt
⅛ tsp. cloves
⅛ tsp. allspice
½ tsp. chili powder
1½ cups long grain rice

Peel the shrimp. Dice or slice the sausage and sauté in the oil and butter over low fire about 5 minutes. Add the onions, green peppers, celery, and garlic and slowly sauté until tender. Stir in thoroughly the tomatoes, seasonings, rice, and water. Add the shrimp and bring to a boil. (To improve your jambalaya, slice the shrimp lengthwise into two.) Reduce the heat and cover. Cook over low temperature for 25 to 30 minutes.

About 5 minutes before the jambalaya is finished, add the green onions and parsley. Cook until the rice is fluffy. This recipe will serve six.

SHRIMP MARENGO

4 lbs. shrimp
8 slices bacon
2 cloves garlic, crushed
1 lb. fresh mushrooms,
  sliced
1 onion, finely chopped
4 tbsp. flour
2 16-oz. cans tomatoes
1 6-oz. can tomato paste
2 cups chicken or beef
  stock

1½ tsp. oregano
1½ tsp. basil
½ tsp. powdered thyme
2 bay leaves
1 tsp. sugar
1 tsp. salt
¼ tsp. black pepper
3 dashes Tabasco
8 tsp. Creole mustard
¼ cup chopped shallots

Cook the shrimp in boiling, salted water for about 6 minutes, then peel and devein. Cut the bacon into small pieces and, in your iron pot or Dutch oven, fry until crisp. Remove the bacon pieces, add the shrimp to the bacon grease, and sauté for 5 minutes.

Add the garlic, mushrooms, and onions and cook for a few minutes longer. Thoroughly mix in the flour. Add the tomatoes, tomato paste, bacon, and stock and bring to a simmer. Season with the oregano, basil, sugar, salt, thyme, bay leaves, pepper, Tabasco, and mustard and mix gently. Allow this to simmer for about 15 minutes. At this point add the shallots and cook for another minute. Taste for seasoning; correct if needed.

Remove from the heat and allow to set for 10 minutes before serving over rice. This dish can be prepared in advance and served later or the following day. It improves the longer you wait. This will serve eight to ten.

Continuing the discussion of the lottery back in my youth, here is some more local history. If you dreamed of your husband, you played 6-41 and 50. If it was your sister, the numbers were 5-15-45. And anytime you dreamed of blood, you played the blood gig, 5-10 and 40.

This all came straight from a highly respected dream book that was passed around by the neighborhood wives. Everybody consulted the dream books before placing bets with their favorite lottery vendors. Just as today racehorse betters have their favorite form sheets, so did the lottery players have their dream interpretation books. (I am of the opinion now that the books were printed and circulated by the lottery companies themselves.) When a particular book was found to give out numbers that would win pretty regularly, its popularity was assured. Memere had her favorite guide, which she consulted practically every morning to translate her dreams into her 10-cent gig and saddle numbers. It was astonishing to realize just how complete these dream books were.

Hundreds of dreams were listed, each with a number value. If a Chinaman entered your dream world the previous night, the next day your bet would be a 10-cent gig and saddle with the numbers 1, 2, 3. If you dreamed about war, all you had to do was play 10-3 and 21. In fact, just about every possible situation in which a human being could be found could be translated into a lottery gig! The most popular bet of all was the famous "washwoman's gig." This was the combination of 4-11-44. More people seemed to play that combination, and somehow it hit a lot more often than other numbers. It hit so often, in fact, that some companies refused to accept the "washwoman's gig" by itself. If you wanted to play that particular combination, you had to add another number to your bet. In other words, you would have to bet on four numbers instead of just three.

If I remember accurately, Memere would play her numbers with two companies, the "Blue Horseshoe" or the "Pelican Lottery Companies." She alternated from one company to the other, depending on how she was winning. If she had a "dry spell" with one company, she would switch and place her money with the other. I remember times when her numbers would "come out." The magnificent sum of $9.46 would be delivered to her that afternoon, and for a few days we lived "high on the hog." Then, as night followed day, the dry spell would follow, so it was back to reality. But during those prosperous "good days," Memere would invest in a few mushrooms, and fix this zesty dish.

SHRIMP MUSHROOM CASSEROLE

½ onion, finely chopped
½ sweet bell pepper, finely
  chopped
4 shallots, finely chopped
4 tbsp. butter
4 tbsp. flour
1½ cups light cream
½ tsp. celery salt
½ tsp. white pepper
½ tsp. paprika

½ tsp. salt
slight pinch of cayenne
  pepper
1 cup grated cheddar
  cheese
¼ lb. mushrooms, sliced
2 lbs. peeled and deveined
  shrimp, cooked in salted
  water
seasoned bread crumbs

Sauté the onion, pepper, and shallots in the butter over low heat until tender. (Do not brown.) Add the flour and mix well. Cook for 3 or 4 minutes.

Add the rest of the ingredients, except the bread crumbs. Stir together and pour into a well-buttered casserole dish. Sprinkle the bread crumbs on top, and bake for about 20 minutes in a preheated 350-degree oven.

Serves six to eight persons.

One of the things Creole cooks knew well (I think it was instinctive with them) was how to cook seafood. Never in a Creole household were you forced to eat fish either overcooked or undercooked. I think Memere would have reserved the hottest places in Hades for anyone who overcooked a piece of tenderloin trout or overpoached a red snapper—by the way, this **POACHED RED SNAPPER** was one of her favorite dishes.

She would begin by making a courtbouillon. A courtbouillon is the seasoned liquid in which fish, shrimp, crab, crawfish, or any other type of seafood are poached. She began with a sliced lemon, some celery tops, shallot tops, a couple of sliced onions, 5 or 6 bay leaves, a dozen or so whole allspice, 1 teaspoon thyme, 1 teaspoon of cayenne pepper, and ½ cup salt. She put these ingredients into about 1½ gallons of water (depending on what she was poaching) and simmered them. The courtbouillon could be used then for boiling any seafood. (Let it boil at least 30 minutes to get the flavor from the seasoning.)

In the meantime, Memere prepared the fish for its "baptism." She took the fish from the icebox and rubbed the exterior with salt. She squeezed some lemon juice over the fish, and let it set while the poaching liquid cooked.

When she was ready, Memere wrapped the fish in enough cheesecloth, so that each end of the cloth was a few inches longer than the fish. She lowered the fish into the simmering liquid. In no more than 20 minutes the fish was cooked. It was gently placed on a platter ringed with fresh lettuce leaves, and when cool, served with a hard-cooked egg salad.

Often, when the shrimp were "running," Memere would fix a dish of **SHRIMP VELOUTÉ** which was "out of this world." First, she boiled 3 pounds of shrimp in salted water, to which she added about ½ teaspoon cayenne pepper. She allowed the shrimp to boil not longer than 10 minutes, and then drained and peeled them. She reserved for later about 2 cups of the liquid the shrimp had boiled in.

Next, Memere sautéed very slowly 1 large finely chopped onion and 1 bunch of chopped shallots. (When I cook this dish, I sauté the onions while I peel the shrimp.) When the onions are very well sautéed, add 4 tablespoons of flour and mix thoroughly. (Do not brown.) Add very slowly, stirring constantly, 2 cups of the reserved liquid. Mix well and begin adding 1 pint of milk. Simmer, then add 1 cup of shredded cheddar cheese, ¼ teaspoon thyme, and salt and pepper to taste. Add the shrimp and cook slowly until the surface begins to look shiny.

Grate about ⅛ teaspoon nutmeg into the sauce and serve over toasted slices of bread.

3 lbs. shrimp
½ tsp. cayenne pepper
2 cups shrimp stock
1 large onion, finely
   chopped
1 bunch shallots, chopped
4 tbsp. flour

1 pt. milk
1 cup shredded cheddar
   cheese
¼ tsp. thyme
salt and pepper to taste
⅛ tsp. nutmeg

RIVERBOAT SHRIMP

1 large green pepper,
  chopped
1 large onion, chopped
2 tbsp. butter
2 No. 2 cans tomatoes
1 tsp. oregano
¼ tsp. rosemary

1 tsp. salt
½ tsp. pepper
3 lbs. shrimp, peeled
¾ cup tomato paste
3 cups cooked rice
1 cup cooked green peas

Sauté the onions and pepper in butter until they are limp. Add the tomatoes and the seasonings and let this simmer for about ½ hour. Add the shrimp, mix well, and cook for 10 minutes. Stir in the tomato paste, and when this is well mixed, add the rice and peas. Heat, stirring often, until steaming hot. Serve immediately.

QUICK SHRIMP NEWBURG

2 cups cooked shrimp
2 tbsp. butter
3 tbsp. flour
¼ tsp. dry mustard

2 tbsp. sherry
salt and pepper to taste
1 cup evaporated milk
¾ cup water

Cut the shrimp in half lengthwise. Melt the butter in a saucepan over very low heat and blend in the flour. When the flour is well blended, add the seasonings and mix well. Remove the pan from the heat and slowly stir in the evaporated milk and water. Cook over a medium heat until the mixture thickens. Remove from heat and stir in the sherry. Add the shrimp, heat thoroughly, and serve.

BUTTERFLY SHRIMP

40 jumbo shrimp
1 pt. milk
1 onion, grated
6 cloves garlic, sliced
1 tsp. Tabasco
2 tbsp. salt

½ tsp. pepper
flour
a few pinches of baking
   powder
cooking oil

Peel the shrimp down to the last joint, leaving the tail and the last joint on. Slice them down the back to the last joint. Put the shrimp into a bowl, then add the grated onion, sliced garlic, and milk. Add the Tabasco, salt, and pepper. Let this marinate for 1 hour. (Two hours would be better.)

Remove the shrimp from the marinade, dry, and dust with flour to which has been added a couple of pinches of baking powder. Fry the shrimp in about 3 inches of hot oil until brown and crisp.

CREVETTES GOURMET

2 lbs. peeled shrimp
7 tbsp. butter
salt and pepper to taste
¼ tsp. Tabasco
1 pkg. frozen asparagus

1½ cups fresh mushrooms,
  sliced
4 medium to large
  tomatoes, peeled,
  seeded, and quartered

WHITE WINE SAUCE

5 tbsp. butter
2 tbsp. flour
1½ cups fish stock
¾ cup dry white wine

4 shallots, finely chopped
3 egg yolks
¼ cup heavy cream
1 tbsp. lemon juice

First, make the white wine sauce. Melt 2 tablespoons of butter, then add the flour. Let cook for 3 to 4 minutes over low heat, stirring constantly. Slowly add the fish stock, stirring all the while. After a couple of minutes of simmering, remove from the heat and set aside for the moment. Simmer the shallots in the wine until the liquid is reduced by half. Soften 1½ tablespoons of the butter and mix in well with the egg yolks. Mix in the reduced wine and put in a pot over a double boiler. Stir until slightly thickened. Work in another 1½ tablespoons butter, stir in the cream and lemon juice, and combine with the butter/flour/fish stock sauce. Heat without boiling.

Fix the frozen asparagus according to the directions on the package; drain. Melt 3 tablespoons butter and sauté the mushrooms until tender. Add the tomatoes and cook for no more than 2 minutes longer. Add the asparagus, and heat over a very low fire for another 2 minutes. Add salt and pepper to taste.

Melt 4 tablespoons butter in a skillet, and add shrimp, a little salt and pepper, and the Tabasco. Cover, and cook gently for about 6 minutes, stirring a couple of times. Arrange the shrimp in a casserole or heatproof serving dish. Spoon over the asparagus/mushroom/tomato mixture and then coat with the white wine sauce. Brown lightly under the broiler just before serving. Serves four to six.

It would be just a few days after Christmas, when returning from the French Market, Memere and I would stop off at the department store to make a few purchases during the after Christmas sales.

Our department store, Rougelot's, had all the virtues of Neiman-Marcus, the clutter of Macy's, and the diversity of Sears Roebuck. Rougelot's handled everything from thimbles to ready-made suits and dresses. The store was located on the corner of Esplanade and Decatur streets. When anything was needed in the way of wearing apparel, shoes, piece goods, and more, we were off to Rougelot's. I remember Memere buying school shirts for me at thirty-five cents and pants for seventy-five cents to one dollar. I remember yellow cotton at ten cents a yard and white cotton material at fifteen cents. What I remember best about our shopping, though, was how Memere bought her shoes.

Right next door to Rougelot's was a little shoe store called Ravin's. After buying what we needed at Rougelot's, we went next door to Ravin's.

Memere weighed just about ninety pounds, and for her size had unusually small feet. Three or four times a year (especially after Christmas), Ravin's had a shoe sale. In the center of the store stood a large table, on which, in glorious disarray, were hundreds of pairs of shoes. The bargain price? Would you believe fifteen cents a pair? Memere went in prepared to try on the shoes. She carried her button hook in her purse. I would bring her the size ones or one-and-one-halfs, and she would sit in a chair and "hook up" one pair after another until she found a pair that suited her. It took a little while to button up and unbutton the shoes. Remember, these shoes went well above the ankle and about twenty buttons had to be unbuttoned. She always managed to find a pair, pay her fifteen cents, and off we went. Figuring about four pairs a year, Memere's shoe expenses amounted to sixty cents a year!

After leaving Ravin's we would often stop at the oyster "saloon" to buy oysters for an oyster stew. Memere had a one-and-one-half quart agate pail she would bring for the oysters. Along with the 4 dozen oysters, she would get as much of the oyster water as the owner of the shop would give her. Once home, she fixed her OYSTER STEW.

OYSTER STEW

4 doz. oysters and oyster
   liquid (Freshly shucked
   oysters are preferred. You
   will notice the difference
   in flavor.)
1 stick butter
1 onion, finely chopped
4 ribs celery, finely chopped
5 tbsp. flour
2 cups water

3 toes garlic, minced
¼ tsp. powdered thyme
1½ pts. milk
dash of pepper sauce
salt and pepper to taste
4 green onions, finely
   chopped
2 tbsp. minced parsley

Melt the butter in an iron pot over a low fire. Add the onions and celery, and sauté them until very soft. Sprinkle in the flour, mix well, and cook for 2 to 3 minutes. Add the water, bring the mixture to a simmer, and cook for another 5 minutes. Add the garlic, thyme, oysters, and oyster liquid. (The oysters and their liquid should add up to about 1½ quarts. Add a little water if necessary to make this amount.) Cook the oysters until the edges begin to curl. Add the milk, salt, pepper, and pepper sauce. Let simmer for a couple of minutes, then add the green onions and parsley.

Remove the stew from the heat. Serves four to six.

OYSTERS BIENVILLE

1 bunch shallots, finely
   chopped
2 tbsp. butter
2 tbsp. flour
½ cup chopped mushrooms
⅔ cup chicken broth
1 egg yolk
ice cream salt
⅓ cup dry white wine

salt and cayenne pepper to
   taste
2 doz. oysters on half shell
½ cup seasoned bread
   crumbs
¼ cup grated Parmesan
   cheese

Sauté the chopped shallots in the butter and slowly stir over a very low heat until the onions are well cooked, but not brown. Sprinkle the shallots with flour and cook until the flour begins to brown. Add the chicken broth and the mushrooms and mix well. Beat the egg yolk into the wine and add to the chicken broth mixture, beating all the while. Season with the salt and cayenne, and cook over a low heat for 15 minutes.

Heat a pan of ice cream salt in a 400-degree oven for 15 minutes. Place the oysters on the half shell in the hot ice cream salt and return to the oven for about 5 minutes. Spoon the sauce over each oyster and sprinkle each with a mixture of the bread crumbs and cheese. Return to the oven and bake until the bread crumb mixture is lightly browned. Two dozen oysters cooked this way will serve four.

OYSTERS IBERVILLE

1 lb. shrimp
1 stick butter
1 bunch shallots, finely
   chopped
½ cup beef consommé
2 doz. oysters and their
   water

1½ cups white wine
Tabasco to taste
seasoned bread crumbs
½ tsp. salt
sprinkle of black pepper

Peel and finely chop the shrimp. Melt the butter in a saucepan and add the shallots. Sauté for a couple of minutes, then add the chopped shrimp, salt, and a sprinkle of black pepper. Cook, while stirring, for five minutes.

In another saucepan, bring the consommé and white wine to a boil. Add the oysters and their water and cook until the edges of the oysters begin to curl. Add a few drops of Tabasco. Put the oysters in the bottom of a casserole and place the shrimp on top. Sprinkle liberally with seasoned bread crumbs which have been mixed with some melted butter. Place the casserole dish under the broiler. When the crumbs are brown, (check after 2 or 3 minutes), the dish is ready to serve. It can be served over buttered toast.

Creole cooking: that incomparable cuisine, developed by those wonderful folks who gave you jambalaya, gumbo, those delectable sauces piquante, crawfish bisque, and many other culinary creations that amaze and stimulate the palates of visitors who come to try our marvelous dishes. Mark Twain once described it (our Creole cooking) as "delicious as the less criminal forms of sin."

Memere, my grandmother, used to say that Creole cooking was a recipe itself. She explained that if you started with a well-seasoned cast iron pot (the blacker the better), added your fat and flour, and stirred carefully for 30 or more minutes, you wound up with a wonderful smelling, nut brown roux. On top of this you dumped a couple of well-chopped onions, some chopped celery, and sweet pepper, sautéed the mixture for a few minutes, and you had the beginning of better than 50 per cent of all Creole dishes.

Of course, it may be argued that with today's modern freezing, canning, precooking, and prepackaging, Creole cooking has become somewhat of an anachronism, but "t'aint so," dear reader. "He who has tasted the wine doesn't return to the grape," and anyone who has savoured our slowly simmered gumbo z'herbes or redfish courtbouillon, or eaten a breakfast of grillades and grits or dipped his French bread into a bowl of chicken and andouille gumbo, becomes an instant convert. You can bet your last beignet that Creole cooking is here to stay, and to further that longevity, here's an old family recipe seeing itself in print for the first time. My mother used this recipe often since it was one of my father's favorites, and so gradually it came to be known as OYSTERS LOUISE.

OYSTERS LOUISE

3 doz. oysters and their
  water (freshly shucked, if
  possible)
½ lb. of artichoke hearts,
  chopped (Marinate them
  in oil.)
½ stick butter
½ cup finely chopped
  shallots

2 tbsp. flour
2 cups milk
2 tbsp. lemon juice
½ tsp. garlic salt
2 dashes Tabasco
salt and pepper to taste
1 pinch grated nutmeg
2 egg yolks

Place the oysters and their juice in a large, heavy skillet. Simmer, on low heat, until the edges of the oysters begin to curl (about 5 minutes). Remove the oysters and roughly chop. In the simmering oyster water, put the butter and shallots and simmer for 5 minutes. Sprinkle the flour into the mixture and cook for 2 or 3 minutes longer. Add the milk slowly, stirring constantly. As the milk begins to simmer, add the oysters, artichoke hearts, lemon juice, garlic salt, Tabasco, salt, and pepper. (This should all be done over low heat.) When the mixture begins to simmer, spoon out about ½ cup of the liquid into a cup. Beat the two egg yolks into the cup. Slowly add this back to the skillet, stirring constantly. Sprinkle with a pinch of nutmeg, and oysters louise is ready.

Served as a side dish or an appetizer, this amount will serve six or eight, depending on the size of their "bon appetit!"

OYSTER EGGPLANT CASSEROLE

2 medium-sized eggplants
1 cup finely chopped onions
4 tbsp. butter or margarine
2 cups bread crumbs
2½ doz. oysters
2 cups oyster water
½ cup finely chopped
   shallots

½ cup light cream
½ tsp. salt
¼ tsp. black pepper
¾ cup grated cheddar
   cheese

Place the eggplants in a 350-degree oven and bake until tender. Check with a fork after about 40 or 45 minutes. If the fork plunges in easily, the eggplants are done. Allow to cool.

Sauté the onions in the butter or margarine for about 10 minutes. Add the bread crumbs and mix well. Remove the mixture from the heat and put it into a bowl. Simmer the oysters in their own water, to which has been added the chopped shallots. Cook for about 5 minutes, or until the oyster edges begin to curl. Remove from heat.

Grease well, with butter or margarine, a 2-quart casserole dish. Peel and slice the eggplant in about ¼-inch slices. Cover the bottom of the dish with half of the eggplant slices. Sprinkle about one third of the onion and bread crumb mixture over the eggplant and pour over this half of the simmered oysters and their juice. Add the remainder of the eggplant, some more bread crumbs, and another layer of the rest of the oysters. Sprinkle the rest of the bread crumbs on top. Pour over the entire mixture the light cream, salt, black pepper, and grated cheddar cheese. Put the casserole into a preheated 350-degree oven and bake for 15 to 20 minutes. Let cool a trifle before serving.

TROUT MARGUERY

4 trout fillets
4 tbsp. olive oil
2 egg yolks
2 sticks butter
1 tbsp. lemon juice
1 cup cooked shrimp,
   chopped

½ cup crabmeat
½ cup sliced mushrooms
2 tbsp. dry white wine
2 drops Tabasco
salt and pepper to taste

Dry the fillets and season with the salt and pepper. Place in a baking dish, add the oil, and bake in a preheated 375-degree oven for about 20 minutes.

While the fish is baking, prepare the sauce. Put the 2 egg yolks in the top of a double boiler over hot, but not boiling, water and beat until slightly thickened. Melt the butter, and slowly add it to the egg yolks, stirring constantly until the mixture thickens. Add the lemon juice, shrimp, crabmeat, mushrooms, wine, and Tabasco. Mix well and season to taste with salt and pepper. Stir and cook for 10 minutes longer.

Place the baked fillets on an oven proof platter. Spoon the sauce over the fish, and run it under the broiler; brown slightly. This will serve four.

POACHED TROUT MARINERE

4 fillets of speckled trout
2 tbsp. lemon juice
1 cup white wine
½ cup butter
1 cup finely chopped
  shallots

3 tbsp. flour
1 pt. milk
1 tbsp. plus ½ tsp. salt
¼ tsp. cayenne
2 egg yolks, beaten
paprika

Put just enough water in a shallow pan to cover the fish. (Do not put the fish in just yet.) Brush the fillets with lemon juice and let stand for 10 minutes. Add 1 tablespoon salt and ⅔ cup of the wine to the water and bring to a simmer. Place the fish carefully in the water and poach for about 10 minutes or until the fish flakes easily. Do not overcook. Remove from the water and place on a heated plate or platter.

In a heavy skillet, melt the butter and sauté the shallots until tender. Blend in the flour, and stirring constantly, cook over a low heat for 4 minutes. Add the milk slowly and stir until smooth. Add ½ tsp. salt, the pepper, and the rest of the wine and cook 10 minutes more. Add the trout and heat through; remove from the heat and stir in the beaten egg yolks.

Put the trout back on the platter and spoon the hot sauce over the top. Sprinkle a little paprika on the dish and heat very briefly under the broiler (a minute or two) until hot. This will serve four.

TROUT MEUNIERE

4 trout fillets
½ cup milk
salt and pepper to taste
1½ sticks clarified butter
1 tbsp. capers

1 tbsp. Worcestershire
  sauce
lemon slices (for garnish)
parsley, minced (for
  garnish)

To clarify the butter, first melt it over low heat. Do not brown. Pour off the clear section, leaving the mild solids to be used in your gumbos or soups. The clear liquid is the clarified butter.

Soak the fish in milk for ½ hour. Drain well and pat dry. Season the fish with salt and pepper and coat with flour. Melt ¼ cup of the butter in a heavy skillet, and brown the fillets on both sides. Remove to a warm platter. Pour the butter out of the skillet and replace with the remaining butter. When hot, add capers and Worcestershire sauce; brown. Pour the sauce over the fillets and garnish with lemon slices and parsley.

CATFISH A LA CREOLE

1 onion, finely chopped	1 small can tomato paste
1 rib celery, chopped	2 thin lemon slices
1 tbsp. minced parsley	1 lb. catfish fillets
2 toes garlic, minced	2 tbsp. lemon juice
¼ cup melted butter	1 tbsp. Worcestershire
1 16-oz. can tomatoes	sauce
¼ lb. mushrooms, sliced	3 tbsp. grated Parmesan
2 bay leaves	cheese
2 dashes Tabasco	salt and pepper to taste

In 2 tablespoons of the butter, slowly sauté the onion, celery, parsley, and garlic until soft. Stir in the tomatoes, mushrooms, bay leaves, Tabasco sauce, tomato paste, and lemon slices. Bring to a boil slowly and then simmer, stirring occasionally, for about 15 to 20 minutes until slightly thickened. Cut the fillets crosswise, into pieces about 2 inches long. Combine with the lemon juice, remaining butter, and Worcestershire sauce and add to the cooking sauce. Stir and add salt and pepper to taste. Cook over low heat for about 10 minutes or until fish flakes. Sprinkle the cheese on top.

This is delicious served with rice. Serves six.

CREOLE CREAMED CATFISH

4 catfish fillets
3 tbsp. butter
¼ cup finely chopped
  shallots
½ cup tomato sauce
2 cups cream

juice of a lemon
2 cups white wine
salt, black, and red pepper
  to taste
⅓ cup finely chopped
  parsley

Salt and pepper the fillets with black pepper and a very light pinch of cayenne pepper. Place them in a heat proof dish with a cover. Mix 3 tablespoons of butter, the shallots, tomato sauce, 1 cup of the cream, the lemon juice, and white wine. Pour this mixture over the fish, cover, and let it simmer slowly for about 20 minutes or until the fillets flake easily. Lift the fish onto a warm platter. Add the other cup of cream and the parsley to the sauce and bring to a boil. Let it cook until the sauce thickens, then pour over the fish. This should serve four.

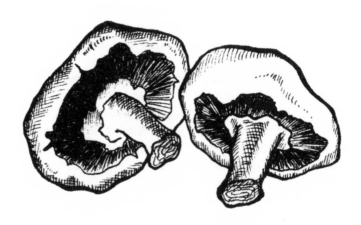

REDFISH CREOLE

1 5-lb. redfish
2 onions, finely chopped
1 green pepper, finely
  chopped
4 stalks celery, finely
  chopped
3 cloves garlic, finely
  chopped
1 6-oz. can tomato paste
1 16-oz. can tomatoes
1 10¾-oz. can chicken
  broth

2 lemons
½ bunch green onions
salt to taste
black pepper to taste
¼ tsp. red pepper
½ tsp. chili powder
½ tsp. basil
6 drops Tabasco
⅓ cup cooking oil
7 tbsp. flour

Clean the redfish, remove the head, make 3 "X-cuts" on each side of the fish, and place it in a large roasting pan. Rub salt and black pepper over the fish, working it into the X-cuts. Squeeze juice from 1 lemon over the fish. Set aside until the sauce is made.

Make a dark brown roux in a heavy iron pot with the cooking oil and flour. Add the chopped onions, pepper, and celery and simmer over low heat until well cooked. When the vegetables are tender, add tomato paste, the can of tomatoes, and the chicken broth. Stir until well blended. Continue cooking over low heat for 5 minutes. Add seasonings, garlic, and salt and black pepper to suit taste. Stir well into the mixture and cook for 10 minutes. Pour the sauce over the redfish.

Place the fish, uncovered, in a preheated 350-degree oven and bake until the fish flakes easily, basting often with the sauce. If more liquid is needed during baking, add more chicken broth. When fish is cooked, place thin slices of lemon along the top. Sprinkle with finely chopped green onions. Serve with rice or potatoes. Serves four to six.

REDFISH COURTBOUILLON

2½ lbs. redfish fillets
5 tbsp. flour
5 tbsp. butter or oil
2 cups chopped onions
1 cup chopped celery
¾ cup chopped bell pepper
3 cloves garlic, minced
½ cup chopped green
 onions
½ cup chopped parsley
1 cup dry white wine

3 cups canned tomatoes,
 drained
2 cups fish stock
½ small can tomato paste
2 tsp. salt
½ tsp. black pepper
4 bay leaves
½ tsp. thyme
2 tbsp. lemon juice
Tabasco to taste

Combine flour and oil (or butter) in a heavy Dutch oven. Cook, stirring constantly, about 15 minutes. Add onions, celery, bell pepper, and garlic. Cook about 10 minutes until brown, stirring occasionally. Mix in the tomatoes and tomato paste. Cook, stirring constantly, about 5 minutes. Add fish stock, wine, parsley, green onions, lemon juice, bay leaves, thyme, salt, pepper, and Tabasco. Simmer about 45 minutes. Add the fish, and simmer 10 to 15 minutes, or until the fish flakes when tested with a fork. Serve with rice.

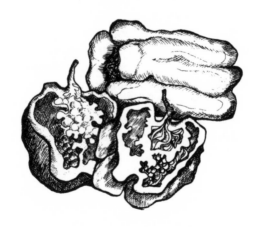

POACHED REDFISH
WITH SEASONED BECHAMEL-EGG SAUCE

4 redfish fillets (about ½ lb. each)
½ stick butter
4 tbsp. flour
2½ cups milk
6 shallots, minced
pinch of grated nutmeg

2 hard-cooked eggs, very finely chopped
2 tbsp. dry white wine
salt and black pepper to taste
2 drops Tabasco

COURTBOUILLON

1 onion, sliced
1 lemon, sliced
5 tbsp. salt
1 tsp. black pepper

4 cloves garlic, sliced
1 tsp. powdered thyme
½ tsp. cayenne pepper
4 bay leaves

First, make a courtbouillon to poach the fish. (A courtbouillon is any seasoned liquid in which seafood is boiled or poached.) Combine all of the courtbouillon ingredients in a couple of quarts of boiling water. Let the liquid boil for about ½ hour after the ingredients have been added, then turn the heat down until the courtbouillon is just barely simmering. Put the fish in and allow to poach approximately 10 minutes. Watch it carefully so it won't overcook. (Check it with a toothpick, and when it breaks apart or flakes, remove carefully from the water and put on a platter.) Let the fish cool completely.

Melt the butter in a heavy skillet over very low heat. Add the shallots and allow to sauté for about 5 minutes. Add the flour, mix well, and while stirring, allow to cook over very low heat for 4 to 5 minutes. Slowly add the milk, stirring until it is well mixed. Allow this to come to a boil, then turn the heat low and let simmer 5 minutes. Add the salt and pepper, wine, Tabasco, and nutmeg. Mix well and taste. Add the chopped eggs, mix into the sauce, and it is ready. Place a fillet on each plate and spoon the sauce over it. This will serve four.

SNAPPER FILLETS A LA BONNE FEMME

8 snapper fillets
1¼ tsp. salt
½ tsp. freshly ground white
  pepper
½ tsp. ground mace
1 cup dry white wine
4 tbsp. butter

½ cup finely chopped
  shallots
1½ cups reserved fish liquor
2 cups warmed milk
1 4-oz. can mushrooms
3 tbsp. flour

Dry the fillets thoroughly and rub with a mixture of salt, pepper, and mace. Roll each fillet into a tight roll and secure with toothpicks; place in an oven proof casserole dish. Preheat the oven to 350°. Pour the wine over the fish and bake for 15 minutes. Pour off the fish liquor and reserve 1½ cups. Cover the fish to keep warm.

In a heavy skillet, melt the butter over a low fire; sauté the shallots for about 3 minutes. Add the flour and cook an additional 3 minutes. Remove from the heat and add the hot fish liquor and the milk. Return to the fire and boil. Simmer slowly for 1 minute, cooking until the sauce is about like heavy cream. Add the mushrooms, and adjust the seasonings if necessary. Pour the sauce over the fillets and serve with rice. Serves six.

BROILED STUFFED FLOUNDER

1 small onion, finely
chopped
½ cup finely chopped celery
½ cup finely chopped green
onions
2 toes garlic, very finely
chopped
½ cup butter (1 stick)
1 cup seasoned bread
crumbs
1½ cups boiled shrimp,
chopped

1½ cups crabmeat (claw
preferably)
2 tbsp. finely chopped
parsley
1 egg, beaten
4 drops pepper sauce
salt and pepper to taste
4 medium-sized flounders
lemon juice

Melt the butter in a heavy saucepan or skillet. Add the onion, celery, green onions, and garlic and sauté for about 5 minutes over low heat. Add the bread crumbs, shrimp, crabmeat, parsley, and egg and mix well. Add the salt, pepper, and pepper sauce and remove from heat.

Take each flounder and make a cut on the thick or dark side down the middle from head to tail, then down the middle crosswise. Loosen the meat from the bone and form a pocket for the stuffing. Brush the inside of the pocket and the rest of the fish with a little melted butter and lemon juice and then stuff the pocket. Place the stuffed fish in a pan with just enough water to cover the bottom. Arrange the fish about 3 inches from the heat and broil until it flakes easily with a toothpick or fork. Baste often with the liquid in the pan. This will serve four.

As summer came to an end, before we had to return to school, Pepere (my grandfather) usually managed to rent a camp at Milneburg. Early on a Saturday morning we would pack up everything we needed for a week on the water. We took the cooking utensils, bedding, some food, our crab nets, and fishing tackle.

By about 9 o'clock in the morning, we were waiting at the corner of Claiborne and Elysian Fields for the train that would take us all the way to the Lakefront. Soon old Smoky Mary would come chugging and whistling from the direction of the river, and with a great letting off of steam would come to a stop for us to board. We scrambled to get on and get our bags and baskets stored away, and then with a toot and ringing of the bell we were off to Milneburg. If everything went well and there were no breakdowns, the trip would take about ½ hour, with one more stop being made at the old Gentilly Road.

When we arrived at Milneburg, we had to unload and cart our bags and baggage to the camp. To get to these camps, we took a long boardwalk that went about a mile along the lakeshore. Each camp, being out in the lake, had its own individual boardwalk running off the main boardwalk. These walks were usually 50 to 100 yards in length. And so we arrived ready for seven or eight glorious days of sunshine, swimming, crabbing, fishing, and eating.

The water around the camp was no deeper than 2 or 3 feet, so the fishing wasn't the greatest. But oh, the crabs we would catch—those big, blue-clawed, fat Lake Pontchartrain crabs! In no time at all we would pull up enough crabs for a "boil" or maybe a gumbo. Sometimes we would pick the meat from a couple of dozen boiled crabs and Memere and Mamete would fix a dozen or so stuffed crabs. When the tide would come in, a few croakers would be caught and these were pan-fried with just a coating of cornmeal.

There were many fulltime fishermen who lived in the area, and during the week they would go from camp to camp in their boats selling their fresh shrimp, croakers, redfish, and speckled trout. The trout was always the favorite, and so for a little or nothing, we had a half dozen or so fresh "specs" to clean, fillet, and cook into that greatest of all trout dishes—AMANDINE.

After the fish were filleted, Memere soaked them in milk for about ½ hour. Try soaking 6 to 8 trout fillets in milk for about 30 minutes. Remove from the milk, dry well, and rub with a little salt and pepper. Dust lightly (and I mean lightly) in flour.

Melt 2 tablespoons of butter in a heavy skillet; add 4 tablespoons oil. When it is hot, sauté the trout, browning lightly on each side. Don't overcook! (Most cooks have a tendency to overcook fish, and this destroys both the texture and the flavor. A good rule of thumb would be no more than 2 minutes for each side, slightly more if the fillets are unusually thick.)

When the fish are lightly browned, remove to a platter. (Be sure the platter has been warmed. This will prevent the fish from getting soggy.)

Pour out the oil and butter in the pan and add 1½ sticks butter. Melt this over low heat and then add ¾ cup slivered almonds. Cook slowly until the almonds are slightly brown, and then add 1 teaspoon Worcestershire sauce, 2 drops of Tabasco sauce, and 2 tablespoons lemon juice. Mix well and pour over the fillets.

Garnish with 2 tablespoons of minced parsley. This should serve six, and with brabant potatoes, is a feast for even the most exacting bon vivant.

TROUT AMANDINE

½ doz. trout fillets
milk (enough to soak the
  fillets)
salt and pepper to taste
flour
1½ sticks plus 2 tbsp.
  butter

4 tbsp. oil
¾ cup slivered almonds
1 tsp. Worcestershire
2 drops Tabasco
2 tbsp. lemon juice
2 tbsp. minced parsley

To continue our discussion of old Milneburg: we were among the hundreds of campers at the Lakefront swimming, fishing, and eating seafood almost every day. Let's stay just a little while longer, so I can describe to you how and where I think Dixieland Jazz originated. At the outset I will admit that there are many theories and accounts of the origin of our jazz not agreeing with what I am going to relate, but nevertheless, I'm writing from personal experience, and the best authority I have is my own eyes and ears.

meats

Milneburg was the "good time" recreation spot for hundreds of New Orleans families. While many families would spend time at the camps during the week, it was on weekends that all merriment would break loose. Early on Saturday mornings the intensity of the celebrating could be forecast by the cases of "home brew" and kegs of beer that were carried along the boardwalk and into the camps—when the foam began to flow, music was needed. Usually, most of the camps had a battered old piano in good enough shape to beat out a few tunes, but musicians were also imported from the city. These musicians were naturals. They were blacks who usually had battered old instruments and no training, but who put their souls into their work. Most of the time the combos were made up of a piano player, a banjo player, and either a clarinet or a cornet player. The real fancy outfits would have the aforementioned four pieces, plus a trombone and a bass horn.

The music would begin on Saturday evenings. The bands played far into the night and half of Sunday. Everybody danced the two-step, and the music fit in perfectly. The tunes? Well, as I said before, these musicians played by ear and the only melodies they knew were the old spirituals. What better jazz tune could be found? As this was repeated year after year, the music developed into Dixieland Jazz, with "Just a Closer Walk with Thee" and "Milneburg Joys" becoming the classics in the jazz bands' repertoire. But the good time would close about Sunday afternoon. A big dinner was served, and then it was time to pack up and get aboard Smoky Mary and head for home.

One of the great dishes we usually had on Sunday was JAMBALAYA. Jambalaya meant "cleaning up the kitchen" with ham, sausage, chicken, shrimp, crab, or anything that was handy. My favorite was a ham and sausage jambalaya that Mamete would fix.

She would use the large (about 10-quart) black iron pot. First, she would slice, in about ½-inch pieces, about 1½ pounds of some good hot sausage. In 3 tablespoons of oil, she would fry the sausage until it was brown. A pound of ham went in next. The ham was diced and sautéed with the sausage and stirred every now and then while she chopped 4 onions, 2 bell peppers, and 4 or 5 ribs of celery. This was added to the pot and allowed to cook until the vegetables were tender. A large can of tomatoes (or if we had the fresh kind, 4 tomatoes chopped) were added to the pot and cooked a few minutes more. Also, she added 6 cups of stock, brought it to a boil, and let it simmer for 30 minutes.

While the pot was simmering, 4 cloves of garlic were chopped and added, along with 4 bay leaves, ¼ teaspoon each of powdered cloves and allspice, 1 sprig of thyme (or she used ½ teaspoon powdered thyme), 1 teaspoon chili powder, and salt and pepper to taste. Both black and cayenne pepper were used, so the jambalaya was "piquante," or very hot!

Then she added 4 cups of raw rice. The jambalaya was brought to a boil and allowed to cook for about 3 minutes, and then the heat was turned very low and the pot covered. After about 15 minutes of cooking, the cover was removed and the mixture was stirred. If the jambalaya seemed dry, more liquid was added. The cover was put back on to cook the mixture for about another 15 or 20 minutes. One bunch of green onions was chopped rather finely and added to the jambalaya during the last 5 minutes of cooking.

The jambalaya was removed from the heat, allowed to set for 5 minutes, fluffed up with a fork, and then served to hungry campers. This served from eight to ten.

HAM AND SAUSAGE JAMBALAYA

1½ lbs. hot sausage
3 tbsp. oil
1 lb. ham, diced
4 onions, chopped
2 bell peppers, chopped
4 or 5 ribs celery, chopped
1 large can tomatoes (or 4 fresh tomatoes, chopped)
6 cups beef or chicken stock
4 cloves garlic, chopped

4 bay leaves
¼ tsp. powdered cloves
¼ tsp. allspice
1 sprig of thyme (or ½ tsp. powdered thyme)
1 tsp. chili powder
salt, black, and cayenne pepper to taste
4 cups raw rice
1 bunch green onions, finely chopped

CREOLE JAMBALAYA

1½ cups rice
1 tbsp. butter
1 slice raw ham
½ lb. chaurice sausage (If not available, use any well-seasoned, smoked sausage.)
1 cup boiled shrimp
1 onion, chopped
2 Creole tomatoes, chopped
1 green pepper, chopped
1 sprig thyme
2 bay leaves
1 pinch cloves
1 tbsp. minced garlic
1 tbsp. minced parsley
1½ pts. beef stock
salt and pepper to taste
cayenne, if desired
½ cup chopped shallots

Cut ham into small pieces. Fry it with the shrimp and chaurice in the butter. Let fry for 10 minutes and then add the onions, green peppers, and the tomatoes. Cook for 5 minutes and add the herbs, garlic, parsley, and the beef stock; boil for 20 minutes. Add salt, pepper, and the rice and cook until rice is almost done. Add the shallots. Cook a little longer and let stand 10 minutes before serving. Serves four to six.

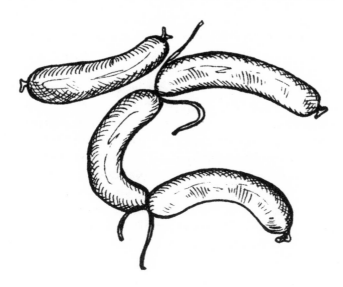

CHICKEN GIZZARD JAMBALAYA

2 tbsp. butter
1 tbsp. oil
1½ lbs. chicken gizzards
1 tsp. salt
1 tsp. black pepper
2 cups chicken stock or
  consommé
2 stalks celery, chopped

2 carrots, chopped
1 onion, chopped
1 cup uncooked rice
1 tbsp. Worcestershire
  sauce
1 cup finely chopped
  shallots
1 tbsp. minced parsley

Heat the butter and oil in a heavy saucepan. Add the gizzards and cook over medium heat until well browned. Add the salt and pepper, stock, and vegetables and let simmer for ½ hour. Add the rice and Worcestershire sauce and simmer, with the pot covered, until the rice is tender and all the stock is absorbed (about 25 minutes). Uncover, add the shallots and parsley, and let steam for 5 to 10 minutes off the burner. This will make four to six servings.

The other day, someone asked me, "What's the difference between Creole and Cajun cooking?" Immediately there flashed into my mind a number of obvious differences, and yet, when I began to make a few comparisons, well . . . .

Of course, it's obvious that both Creoles and Cajuns take food—its freshness, its presence, and its preparation—just about as seriously as they take anything on earth. Some say the difference is between "city cooking" and "country cooking." But they are both French cooking, aren't they? Well, not exactly. Actually, it's not strictly French cooking at all. Remember the Spanish, Indian, and black influences. All right, so Cajun cooking is spicier than Creole—sometimes, not always. Cajuns like a lot of rice—but the Creoles ate a lot of rice, too! The best way I can describe the difference for the most part is in the serving. The Creoles eat in the dining room while the Cajuns eat in the kitchen—but not always!

One thing the Cajuns should be praised for is the way they have developed the art of sausage making. Once you have tasted andouille, chaurice, boudin rouge, boudin blanc, or saucisse boucaner, you've got to go back for more, and I've named but a few. Both the Creoles and the Cajuns used these delicious sausages in soups, vegetable dishes, in gumbos, and of course served by themselves.

One of the favorite uses is in a jambalaya. Here is an easy, quick way to whip up a tasty **SAUSAGE JAMBALAYA.**

You will need about a pound or a pound and a quarter of chaurice, smoked sausage, or andouille. Slice the sausage into small pieces, then brown in a deep frying pan or Dutch oven. Take the meat out and put into the same fat, 2 large onions, chopped, ½ cup finely chopped celery, and one chopped bell pepper. Sauté until tender. Mix in thoroughly 1 large can of tomatoes. Add 2 bay leaves, ½ teaspoon basil, ½ teaspoon thyme, ½ teaspoon chili powder, and 4 toes chopped garlic. Mix well and add 1 10½-oz. can of beef consommé and 2 cans of water. Let simmer for about 40 minutes.

Put the sausage back, and add salt, black pepper, and Tabasco to taste. Add 2 cups raw rice. Put a cover on and allow the mixture to cook slowly, stirring occasionally. As the rice begins to absorb the mixture, the jambalaya might get too dry. If so, add a little more water. Cook until the rice is tender.

Just before serving, stir into the jambalaya ½ cup finely chopped shallots and 2 tablespoons minced parsley. Let set for 10 minutes, then serve with a big chunk of French bread and butter. Serves four to six.

1 or 1¼ lbs. chaurice, smoked sausage, or andouille
2 large onions, chopped
½ cup finely chopped celery
1 bell pepper, chopped
1 large can tomatoes
2 bay leaves
½ tsp. basil
½ tsp. thyme
½ tsp. chili powder
4 toes garlic, chopped
1 can beef consommé
2 cans water
salt, black pepper, and Tabasco to taste
2 cups raw rice
½ cup finely chopped shallots
2 tbsp. minced parsley

SAUSAGE AND EGGPLANT JAMBALAYA

1 lb. good sausage
1 large onion, finely
   chopped
1 bell pepper, finely
   chopped
3 ribs celery, finely chopped
4 cloves garlic, minced
1½ cups uncooked rice
3 cups chicken or beef
   stock or water
couple of dashes of pepper
   sauce

2 bay leaves
½ tsp. powdered thyme
½ tsp. chili powder
salt and pepper to taste
2 medium-sized eggplants,
   peeled and cut into ½-in.
   cubes
6 green onions, finely
   chopped

In a heavy pot, fry the sausage after slicing it into rounds about ¼ inch thick. Stir frequently, and when lightly browned remove the sausage and reserve. Pour off all but about ¼ cup of the fat and add the onions, bell pepper, and celery. Cook until the vegetables are soft. Add the rice and mix well until the grains are evenly coated. Add the stock or water, the garlic, pepper sauce, bay leaves, thyme, chili powder, and salt and pepper, and bring to a boil. Add the sausage and the cubed eggplant and lower the heat. Partially cover the pot and cook over low heat for about 45 minutes. Toward the end of the cooking procedure the rice should absorb most of the liquid. If it becomes too dry a little liquid may be added, a few tablespoons at a time. When almost cooked, stir in the green onions and mix well. Serve when hot. This should serve four.

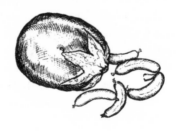

A very important aspect of Creole cooking is a careful selection of the ingredients. This care and attention in choosing ingredients was very much in evidence when a Creole housewife went shopping or, as she expressed it, "made her marketing." She went shopping with her eyes, nose, and fingers! She painstakingly checked quality and compared values. To the uninitiated, it would have been a gratifying experience to accompany one of these housewives on her early morning buying trip.

As the Creole housewife left for the market, she knew what she wanted and just where to find it. She started out just after daybreak. If she waited any later, she knew she would have to select from "leavings." With a basket on her arm, she went off to market. I always accompanied Memere on her three or four times a week trip to the French Market, so I knew the routine exactly.

If Memere decided on poultry, we went first to the chicken cages where a "live" selection was made. The attendant pulled the chicken out of the cage, and while he held it by the feet, Memere examined it from beak to toenails! (Let me backtrack a moment to explain that even before the chicken was chosen, Memere would observe the fowl in their cages. If the bird was the least bit droopy, it was never selected.) With her fingers, Memere felt the chicken for firmness of flesh and fat. She would then wiggle the end of the breastbone, a way of determining the chicken's age. The more flexible the end of the bone, the younger and more tender the chicken. Then the bird would be killed, plucked, and drawn.

If it were beef or veal she was after, the same assiduous care went into the selection. The piece she desired would be cut from a larger piece Memere had smelled and felt before she made her selection. If fish were on the menu, the creatures were examined to determine if the eyes were clean and bright, the gills red, and the smell fresh. The vegetables were pored over, with careful attention given to their color, firmness, and fresh looks.

Having obtained the best possible raw materials, the Creole cook headed home to work on the meals for the day. Back in the kitchen, she directed her efforts to bringing out the full flavor of her fresh ingredients. The recipe that follows is a case in point. Fix it with the best and most fresh ingredients, and your enjoyment is assured—but of course, the opposite is also predictable. The Creoles called it "Viande Au Jus"—we know it today as **STEAK TARTARE.**

Have the butcher grind 1½ pounds of fresh top round or sirloin, after trimming away as much of the fat as he can. With this you'll need 3 egg yolks from 3 fresh eggs. If you can't get fresh eggs, skip the whole thing. Mix in gently, with your hands, the 3 fresh yolks with the fresh meat. Next, add 1 cup finely chopped onion, ¼ cup chopped shallots, 2 tablespoons Creole mustard, 1 tablespoon lemon juice, 4 tablespoons olive oil, 1 teaspoon salt, ½ teaspoon black pepper, a pinch of powdered thyme, a pinch of powdered cloves, and 1 tablespoon finely minced parsley. Mix all the ingredients gently with your hands, then cover and chill in the refrigerator for 15 minutes. This amount will make four portions.

Serve on crisp lettuce leaves with a garnish of dill pickle. Fresh— and oh so good!

1½ lbs. fresh top round or
    sirloin, ground
3 egg yolks
1 cup finely chopped onion
¼ cup chopped shallots
2 tbsp. Creole mustard
1 tbsp. lemon juice

4 tbsp. olive oil
1 tsp. salt
½ tsp. black pepper
pinch of powdered thyme
pinch of powdered cloves
1 tbsp. finely minced
    parsley

STEWED KIDNEYS

1 cup finely chopped onions
3 cloves garlic, chopped
½ green pepper, chopped
4 shallots, chopped
½ stick butter
1 cup beef stock or canned
    beef bouillon

2 bay leaves
4 veal kidneys
salt and pepper to taste
1 tbsp. flour
1 cup apple cider vinegar
1½ cups red wine

First, cut the kidneys into small pieces, discarding all fat, and soak overnight in a mixture of 1 cup apple cider vinegar and 1 cup red wine.

Drain the kidneys. Melt the butter in a heavy saucepan and sauté the onions, garlic, and pepper over a low fire until the vegetables are tender. Sprinkle the flour in the pan and add a cup of beef stock or canned beef bouillon and the bay leaves. Simmer a few minutes and add the drained kidneys. Let simmer for 10 minutes before adding ½ cup of red wine and the shallots. Salt and pepper to taste and simmer 10 more minutes.

Serve over rice. Serves four.

VEAL KIDNEYS AND RICE

6 veal kidneys
2 tbsp. butter
2 onions, chopped
1 cup beef consommé
1 small ripe tomato,
    chopped

1 tsp. flour
2 tsp. Creole mustard
3 cups hot cooked rice

Soak kidneys in cold water for 1 hour. Drain, pat dry, and cut across into thin slices.

Melt the butter in a heavy frying pan and add the kidneys and onions. Cook and stir over a fairly high heat for 3 minutes. Pour in the consommé, add the tomato, and cook, stirring often, for about 5 minutes. Mix the flour and mustard to a smooth paste and stir this into the pan. Blend well, then remove from heat and mix gently with the hot rice.

Serve at once. This will make four to six servings.

ORANGE-GLAZED PORK CHOPS

4 rib pork chops, cut 1½ in.
  thick, each with a pocket
  (2 lbs. total)

STUFFING:

3 tbsp. butter or margarine
½ cup finely chopped onion
½ cup chopped celery
¼ cup chopped green
  onions
1½ cups soft bread cubes

2 tbsp. chopped parsley
1 tsp. salt
½ tsp. grated orange peel
1½ tsp. seasoned salt
3 tbsp. orange juice

GLAZE:

½ cup orange juice
¼ cup light brown sugar

¼ cup orange marmalade
2 tbsp. cider vinegar

Preheat the oven to 375°. Wipe pork chops well.

Cook the onions, green onions, and celery in hot butter until tender (about 8 minutes). Add bread cubes and brown slightly. Remove from heat. Add parsley, salt, orange peel, 1 teaspoon of the seasoned salt, and orange juice; toss mixture lightly to combine.

Fill the pockets of the chops with the stuffing. Stand chops on rib bones on a rack in a shallow roasting pan. Sprinkle with ½ teaspoon seasoned salt. Pour water to ½-inch depth in the roasting pan. (The water should not touch the rack.) Cover chops and roasting pan with foil. Bake chops 1½ hours.

Meanwhile, prepare the glaze. Combine all of the ingredients in a small saucepan, mixing well. Bring to the boiling point, stirring constantly. Reduce heat and simmer, uncovered, 15 minutes.

Remove the foil from the chops and pour off the water. Brush the chops with some of the glaze. Bake, uncovered, 30 minutes or until the chops are tender and brown. Baste with the glaze every 10 minutes. Makes four servings.

One of the truly great, classic breakfast dishes concocted by those wonderful folks who gave us jambalaya, gumbo, and courtbouillon (the Creoles, who else?) is grillades and grits.

Let's start by using the correct pronunciation for grillades. It's pronounced "gree-yahds"—no "L" sound whatsoever. The pronunciation for g-r-i-t-s I leave to your own ingenuity. Grillades was a dish that I remember Memere and Mamete fixed often, particularly during the winter months. I used to enjoy watching the meat being pounded, and then, after the grillades were cooking and the pot was covered so that I could watch no longer, my attention would be attracted by the grits. I would be fascinated watching the thick white bubbles and hearing the plopping noise they made as they surfaced and broke. Of course, we not only ate the grillades for breakfast; often we had them for supper, and we always considered it a treat to eat the tender, juicy morsels of meat and "sop up" the dark, reddish-brown gravy with our grits.

Of course, the way those Creole gals cooked and seasoned the grits, you really didn't need anything else with it. I'll tell you how they did it later, but for now, let's have a go at the grillades. This recipe, by the way, was Mamete's own original combination, and I have never seen any quite like it.

The first thing to do is combine 2 teaspoons of salt with 1 teaspoon black pepper, ¼ teaspoon cayenne pepper, and 4 to 5 cloves of garlic, very finely chopped. Be sure all the ingredients are well mixed. Next, take about 1½ to 1¾ pounds of veal or beef round and cut the meat into 2-inch squares. Be sure to trim off all fat, gristle, or bone. Take a tenderizer—you know, the thing with the prongs and handle—and begin to pound each square of meat. You must pound until each square almost doubles in size.

When you are about halfway through each square, dip the tenderizer into the mixture of seasonings and garlic, and pound this into the meat, one dip for each side. When the meat is pounded, rub it on each side with a little flour.

Now we're ready to fry it. Put 2 tablespoons butter and 1 tablespoon oil in a Dutch oven; brown the meat on each side. When the meat is brown, remove to a platter. Add to the oil 1½ cups chopped onions, ½ cup finely chopped celery, and ½ cup finely chopped green pepper.

Cook, stirring constantly, until the vegetables are tender. Return the meat to the pot and add one 16-ounce can of tomatoes and 1¼ cups water; turn the heat to low.

Cover and simmer for about 1 hour, or until the meat is tender. You can hasten the tenderizing process by adding 1 tablespoon vinegar to the pot.

Now for the grits. Buy a package of the old-fashioned kind requiring ½ hour or so of cooking; follow the directions to the letter. You will need about 2 cups of grits to serve with the grillades, so again, observe the directions on the package.

After the grits are cooked, add ½ stick of butter and 1 raw egg and beat well. Salt to taste and eat to your heart's content. Serve the gravy, of course, over the meat and grits. This should serve four to six.

GRILLADES

2 tsp. salt
1 tsp. black pepper
¼ tsp. cayenne pepper
4 to 5 cloves garlic, very finely chopped
1½ to 1¾ lbs. veal or beef round, cut into 2-in. squares
flour

2 tbsp. butter
1 tbsp. oil
1½ cups chopped onions
½ cup finely chopped celery
½ cup finely chopped green pepper
1 16-oz. can tomatoes
1¼ cups water
1 tbsp. vinegar (optional)

GRITS

1 pkg. old-fashioned grits
½ stick butter

1 egg
salt to taste

I really believe that one of the very strong reasons why Memere and Mamete were great Creole cooks was because neither one had any psychological hang-ups about food. Memere used to say, "A person who appreciates good food will eat anything that walks, swims, or flies." Mamete used to modify that expression by adding "if properly fixed."

Maybe this explains why, at a very early age, I was already accustomed to eating such dishes as stewed or broiled kidneys, boiled tongue, fried brain, tripe, heart, liver, and many other dishes to which our modern children have grown so unaccustomed.

I remember very well watching Memere or Mamete as they would kill, pluck, clean (we called it gut), and cook a chicken, or skin, clean, and dismember a rabbit or two, while a sauce piquante was simmering away, waiting to be introduced to the meat that would cook to a delicious tenderness.

It soon came natural to me to grab a chicken from the yard, behead it, and after it had finished jumping, dip it into a tub of very hot water and pluck the feathers. Then a cut was made crosswise below the breastbone, and the chicken was left with nothing but a clean cavity. One of the things we youngsters prized was the "craw," a thin skin bag taken from the neck area, cleaned, and used as a balloon. A craw had two tubes. We tied one with a piece of string and blew up the craw! I wonder how many of today's children have ever seen a craw balloon?

One of the real economical dishes we enjoyed was chitterlings. (Notice I spelled it "chitter" even though we pronounced it "chittlin.")

Memere used to say she could tell by a way a person pronounced it whether he would eat it. I think maybe some people were turned off because "chittlins" didn't smell too great while they were cooking (neither does sauerkraut, but who will deny it is delicious?). Anyone who has never eaten chittlins owes it to himself to at least try it once.

Buy a pound of chittlins and wash them well. (To clean them well, turn them inside out and pull most of the fat out.) Put about 2½ quarts of water on to boil, add a little salt and pepper, and boil the meat until tender.

Sometimes chittlins are served hot with a little butter, salt, and pepper. Or you might sprinkle them with a little tarragon vinegar, salt, and pepper and eat between slices of French bread. If you really want to fix your chittlins in a most delicious way, after they are boiled, remove from the water and drain well. Coat with seasoned flour (salt and pepper, a pinch of thyme, and a pinch of chili powder). Dip in a beaten egg and roll in cracker crumbs. Melt a couple of tablespoons of bacon grease in your skillet and fry the chittlins until crisp. With a chunk of French bread and a cold draught beer, mon ami, those chittlins are great!

CHITTLINS I

1 lb. chittlins
2½ qts. water
salt and pepper to taste

butter
tarragon vinegar (if desired)

CHITTLINS II

1 lb. chittlins
2½ qts. water
salt and pepper to taste
seasoned flour (Season with
salt and pepper, a pinch
of thyme, and a pinch of
chili powder.)

1 egg, beaten
cracker crumbs
a few tbsp. bacon grease

There were times when Memere would grudgingly admit that some very good dishes were not necessarily classified as part of the Creole "grand cuisine." She would quickly retort, however, that they had somehow been influenced by the Creoles or were offshoots of the New Orleans style of cooking. Most of these dishes she identified as "home cooking," to distinguish them from the haute cuisine of Louisiana. Today we call it "soul food," and a mighty good food it is, too!

To pinpoint what soul food really is, let's first identify it as a unique style of cooking more indigenous to this country than any other American cooking style. It evolved entirely without any European influence, unlike the Creole, which was a mixture of French, Spanish, Indian, and African, with a little Italian, German, and English thrown in for good measure. (How international can you get?) Soul food is an honest, down-to-earth type of cuisine with no frills. It is delicious, and a marvelous example of what good southern black cooks could do with much less than an ideal selection of ingredients.

In his excellent little *Soul Food Cook Book*, Bob Jeffries relates how "soul food, like jazz, was created in the South by American blacks and although it can safely be said that almost all typically southern food is 'soul'—the word soul, when applied to food, means only those foods that blacks grew up eating in their own homes; food that was cooked with care and love, with soul, by and for themselves, their families and friends."

Memere described "home cooking" as having been developed by people "short on money and long on creativity." How right she was when one considers that from soul cooking came such delights as hogshead cheese, hoppin' john, dubie, sweet potato pone, and cracklin. But let's stop defining and explaining and get down to the eating part, with two classic soul dishes, "HOPPIN' JOHN" and "GIZZARD STEW."

For the HOPPIN' JOHN, first you take a pound of black-eyed peas and soak them overnight in water. Put 8 slices of bacon, cut into fourths, in a heavy pot and fry until crisp. Add 1½ cups finely chopped onions and cook until the onions are transparent. Add 2½ quarts of water and bring to a boil. Add 2 cloves minced garlic, ⅛ teaspoon cayenne, ⅛ teaspoon thyme, 1 bay leaf, ⅛ teaspoon rosemary, ½ teaspoon salt, and ¼ teaspoon black pepper.

Drain the black-eyed peas and add to the boiling mixture. Partially cover the pot and lower the heat so that it is barely simmering. Cook for 1½ hours, and then add 2 cups raw rice. Let this cook for 30 minutes, until the peas and rice are tender, then serve with hunks of crisp French bread.

Now, let me tell you about the GIZZARD STEW. Rough chop (that means don't chop too fine) 2 pounds of chicken gizzards and put into a large, heavy saucepan with 2 tablespoons butter and 1 tablespoon oil. Cook over a moderate heat until the giblets are browned. Add 1 cup chopped onions, ½ cup chopped celery, and ½ cup chopped carrots; sauté for 5 minutes. Sprinkle with ½ teaspoon salt and ½ teaspoon black pepper. Add 2 cups of chicken stock and 1 tablespoon Worcestershire sauce, mix well, and bring to a boil.

Add 1¼ cups uncooked rice, lower the heat so the pot quietly simmers, and partially cover and cook until the rice is tender and the liquid has been absorbed. Add ¾ cup finely chopped shallots, mix well, and you are ready for a real treat.

HOPPIN' JOHN

1 lb. black-eyed peas
8 slices bacon, cut into
    fourths
1½ cups finely chopped
    onions
2½ qts. water
2 cloves garlic, minced

⅛ tsp. cayenne
⅛ tsp. thyme
1 bay leaf
⅛ tsp. rosemary
½ tsp. salt
¼ tsp. black pepper
2 cups raw rice

GIZZARD STEW

2 lbs. chicken gizzards,
  roughly chopped
2 tbsp. butter
1 tbsp. oil
1 cup chopped onions
½ cup chopped celery
½ cup chopped carrots

½ tsp. salt
½ tsp. black pepper
2 cups chicken stock
1 tbsp. Worcestershire
1¼ cups uncooked rice
¾ cup finely chopped
  shallots

HOPPIN' JOHN JAMBALAYA

1 cup chopped onions
1 bunch shallots, chopped
1 bell pepper, chopped
¼ cup chopped parsley
3 cloves garlic, chopped
3 tbsp. vegetable oil
1 lb. salt meat, boiled for 15
  minutes and cut into
  small pieces

2 lbs. smoked hot sausage,
  sautéed and cut into
  small pieces
1 lb. black-eyed peas,
  boiled until about half
  done
1½ cups uncooked rice
6 cups chicken broth
salt and pepper to taste

Sauté onions, pepper, garlic, and parsley in oil. Cook for about 10 minutes on a moderate fire. Add the salt meat, sausage, black-eyed peas, chicken broth, and salt and pepper to taste. Bring to a boil and add the rice. When the mixture boils again, cover tightly and cook for 45 minutes on a very low heat. Do not uncover during this time.

Remove cover, add the chopped shallots, and mix well. Let set for 5 to 10 minutes before serving. Serves six to eight.

CREOLE LASAGNE

1 box lasagne noodles, boiled
tomato sauce (See recipe.)
white wine and onion sauce (See recipe.)
2 cups well-seasoned, cooked spinach

1½ cups grated cheese (mixture of Parmesan and Swiss)
3 cups browned ground beef or pork
½ cup cottage cheese

TOMATO SAUCE

1 large white onion, minced
2 tbsp. olive oil
2 large tomatoes, peeled, seeded, and chopped
2 cups Italian plum tomatoes (No. 1 can)
¼ tsp. powdered thyme
1 tsp. basil

1 bay leaf
3 cloves garlic, minced
¼ tsp. cloves
¼ tsp. allspice
½ tsp. oregano
salt and pepper to taste
2 dashes Tabasco

WHITE WINE AND ONION SAUCE

½ cup minced onions
8 tbsp. butter
8 tbsp. flour
3½ cups hot milk

½ cup dry white wine or French vermouth
½ cup chopped mushrooms
salt and pepper to taste

To prepare the tomato sauce, first slowly sauté the onions in olive oil until tender. Stir in the fresh tomatoes, cover, and cook slowly for 5 minutes. Add the seasonings, salt, and pepper, and let simmer while you drain and mash the plum tomatoes. (Reserve the juice.) Add the plum tomatoes and cook for 30 minutes, adding a little juice from the can of tomatoes if the sauce becomes too thick.

For the white wine and onion sauce, first sauté the onions in the butter for about 3 minutes, then add the flour. Cook slowly over a very low heat for 3 minutes, then slowly add the hot milk, stirring until well

CREOLE LASAGNE

1 box lasagne noodles,
  boiled
tomato sauce (See recipe.)
white wine and onion sauce
  (See recipe.)
2 cups well-seasoned,
  cooked spinach

1½ cups grated cheese
  (mixture of Parmesan and
  Swiss)
3 cups browned ground
  beef or pork
½ cup cottage cheese

TOMATO SAUCE

1 large white onion, minced
2 tbsp. olive oil
2 large tomatoes, peeled,
  seeded, and chopped
2 cups Italian plum
  tomatoes (No. 1 can)
¼ tsp. powdered thyme
1 tsp. basil

1 bay leaf
3 cloves garlic, minced
¼ tsp. cloves
¼ tsp. allspice
½ tsp. oregano
salt and pepper to taste
2 dashes Tabasco

WHITE WINE AND ONION
SAUCE

½ cup minced onions
8 tbsp. butter
8 tbsp. flour
3½ cups hot milk

½ cup dry white wine or
  French vermouth
½ cup chopped mushrooms
salt and pepper to taste

To prepare the tomato sauce, first slowly sauté the onions in olive oil until tender. Stir in the fresh tomatoes, cover, and cook slowly for 5 minutes. Add the seasonings, salt, and pepper, and let simmer while you drain and mash the plum tomatoes. (Reserve the juice.) Add the plum tomatoes and cook for 30 minutes, adding a little juice from the can of tomatoes if the sauce becomes too thick.

For the white wine and onion sauce, first sauté the onions in the butter for about 3 minutes, then add the flour. Cook slowly over a very low heat for 3 minutes, then slowly add the hot milk, stirring until well

they had had to accept what is packaged and displayed at meat counters today. Incidentally, there is one supermarket chain advertising they put the best side of the meat *down* when it is packaged. Don't you believe it. This has been tested and found wanting. If you are being fooled through spurious packaging, take the meat back.

With a fine beef roast, always remember that the larger and heavier the roast, the lower the oven temperature should be. This may sound like a contradiction, but it really makes sense. You see, since a large roast has to be cooked longer, a high temperature would overcook the outside before the inside was really ready. For a 10 to 12 pound roast, try cooking it at 275° to 300° and find out how much more succulent the meat will be. On small 3 to 6 pound roasts, try using 375° to 400° temperatures.

How do you tell when a roast is about done? Memere had a really intriguing way. She would take a skewer and stick it all the way into the center of the roast. She would leave it in for 1 minute, and then test by applying the skewer to her lip. If the part that was in the center was hot, the entire roast was well done, if just warm, the center would be rare, and if almost cool, the roast was very rare.

Before we leave the beef roast, remember it is very important to first dry a roast very well before putting it in the oven; it will brown much nicer. Never, never stick a roast with a fork to turn it; the juices come pouring out! Also, after a roast is cooked, always, before slicing, allow the meat to set for at least 10 minutes.

Now, let's turn to veal, the meat most used by the Creole cooks, and try a dish Memere used to call "MIGNONNETTES." I think the real name was "Mignonnettes de Veau Normandes."

You will need one veal round, 1½ to 2 pounds. Cut the round into four sort of rectangular pieces and try to shape each piece into an oval, or mignonnette, with your fingers. You might have to trim a few corners with the knife in order to get the oval shape.

Sprinkle the meat with a little salt and black pepper. Slap a few times with the flat of the knife and then dust lightly with flour. Melt ¾ stick of butter in a heavy frying pan. When the butter is hot, add the veal and about ½ pound sliced mushrooms.

Cook this on a rather low heat for 10 minutes, turning the meat over a few times while stirring the mushrooms. When the veal is browned, take it out and place on plates that have been warmed in a 200-degree oven.

Add ½ cup Calvados (apple brandy) to the butter and mushrooms and mix thoroughly. Add a pinch of black pepper and 2 or 3 pinches of salt. Turn the heat very low and add 1 cup of heavy cream. Stir the cream well into the mixture, and raise the heat a little to a simmer. Keep it simmering until the sauce thickens slightly.

Now you are ready to serve. In each plate, spoon the sauce over the mignonnettes and enjoy! This should serve four eager eaters.

VEAL MIGNONNETTES

1½ to 2 lbs. veal round
salt and black pepper
flour (enough to dust the veal)
¾ stick butter

½ cup Calvados (apple brandy)
1 cup heavy cream
½ lb. sliced mushrooms

EASY PATE

1 pkg. (about 12 oz.) braunschweiger or liverwurst
3 strips bacon, fried until crisp, drained, and finely chopped

¼ cup minced onions
4 green onions, minced
¼ cup chopped black olives
½ cup mayonnaise
garlic salt and black pepper to taste

Combine all the ingredients and mix well. Refrigerate for at least 1 hour to allow the flavors to mingle. Serve on crackers, toast, or bread.

Whenever Memere decided to make hogshead cheese, we would leave very early in the morning for the French Market. We returned with half a hogshead and about 10 pounds of assorted bones in the market basket. That half a head cost fifteen cents and the bones were free. She would make head cheese five or six times a year, always in the fall and winter. Refrigeration facilities being what they were, she never made hogshead cheese during hot weather. The whole operation, from beginning to end, took about 12 hours, and the cheese wasn't ready to eat until the following day.

When we returned home with the meat and the bones, we went to work to build a charcoal fire. The charcoal was burned in the type of furnace the average housewife used to boil her clothes. About twice a month, when the white clothes began to yellow or show a tinge of gray, they were ready to be boiled. The clothes were all dumped into a kettle of water and, with a bit of soap added, were boiled a few hours. Then they were dipped into blueing water and hung to dry, their whiteness restored.

Back to the head cheese. When the charcoal fire was glowing, the kettle, with about 5 gallons of water and all the meat, was put on top. After a few hours of simmering, the hogshead was removed, stripped of the meat, and finely chopped. The bones were allowed to boil a few hours more. Then the bones were removed and the chopped pork from the head was returned to the kettle.

Chopped onions, shallots, celery, green peppers, and garlic were added, and everything was cooked a few more hours. Then came the pepper. This cheese was very hot and seasoned in a special way. Memere would boil a couple of long red peppers a few hours in a small pot, and then added them to the kettle, a tablespoon at a time, constantly tasting. To give the cheese that wonderful dark brown color, Memere burned sugar in her skillet and added it to the kettle. Late in the evening, the kettle would be lifted off and allowed to cool.

What a wonderful aroma filled the kitchen as we waited until the cheese was ready to pour. When it had cooled sufficiently we would "dipper" it out into bowls and put it back in the icebox. As the saying goes, "make a better hogshead cheese and the neighborhood soon finds out." People came from far and near the next day just to get the little bowls of hogshead cheese—and who could blame them? But, let's face it, who would go through all that trouble today? So, let's try a dish very similar, but oh, so much easier.

This is a version of the classic CREOLE DAUBE GLACÉ. Take 1 cup of finely shredded cooked meat (such as roast or soup meat) and about 20 stuffed, sliced olives. In molds, place the olives on the bottom and put the chopped meat on top. Heat 1 can of beef consommé and dissolve 2 packages of unflavored gelatin in it. Add to this another can of consommé, 1 bunch green onions, minced, 2 tablespoons finely chopped parsley, 3 cloves garlic, finely chopped, 2 tablespoons Worcestershire sauce, 3 good shakes of Tabasco sauce, and salt and pepper to taste. Mix well and pour over the meat in the molds. Refrigerate until hard; there you have another Creole specialty.

CREOLE DAUBE GLACÉ

1 cup finely shredded cooked meat (roast or soup meat)
20 stuffed, sliced olives
2 10½-oz. cans beef consommé
2 pkgs. unflavored gelatin
1 bunch green onions, minced

2 tbsp. finely chopped parsley
3 cloves garlic, finely chopped
2 tbsp. Worcestershire
3 good shakes Tabasco
salt and pepper to taste

DAUBE GLACÉ

2⅛ to 3 lbs. beef round
2⅛ lbs. veal rump
veal shank or 2 or 3 pig's
   feet
¼ lb. salt meat
6 carrots, thinly sliced
3 cups minced onions
1 cup minced scallions
1 turnip, diced
5 cloves garlic
3 bay leaves

1 tsp. powdered thyme
¼ tsp. powdered cloves
¼ tsp. powdered allspice
2 tbsp. minced parsley
¼ tsp. cayenne
salt and black pepper to
   taste
½ tbsp. thyme
1 onion, chopped
1 cup sherry
shortening or cooking oil

Cut the salt meat into strips about ⅛ of an inch thick and roll the strips into the cayenne, powdered thyme, parsley, allspice, and cloves. Make slits in the beef round and force the salt meat and the spices into the slits. Rub the meat with salt and black pepper and then in a heavy skillet, brown in a little shortening or oil. When brown, add enough hot water to cover, along with 2 bay leaves, 3 cloves garlic, minced, the carrots, turnips, minced onions, and scallions. Cover and simmer slowly 2 or 3 hours, or until the meat is tender.

Rub a little salt and pepper into the veal rump and place in enough water to cover along with the shank or pig's feet. Add the 1 bay leaf, thyme, 2 cloves garlic, 1 chopped onion, and sherry. Boil until the meat will fall off the bone. Remove meat from the bone and mince very fine. Return meat to the sauce and season well with salt and pepper. Pour the sauce over the cooked daube, allow to cool, and refrigerate.

You can serve the next day, cold, cutting the meat and jelly into thin slices. Serves four to six.

A good turtle soup is usually the way most of us are introduced to turtle meat. Seldom, if ever, do we have the opportunity to savor any other turtle dishes, and yet one of the truly great Creole dishes, believe it or not, was TURTLE STEW! Often, returning from the French Market with a few pounds of turtle meat, Memere, knowing the whole family's liking for it, would fix her turtle stew.

Any good Creole cook would have felt very comfortable in her kitchen, and would have enjoyed going through the daily cooking routine. In a corner of the room stood the black, cast iron stove, and occupying about half of one wall was a huge fireplace unused for many years. Inside the fireplace was stacked the wood for the stove. In a little box in front of the wood was the "kindlin," the thin slivers of wood that would ignite easily and which we used to start the fire in the morning. Above the fireplace was a thick piece of timber serving as a kind of mantle place, where Memere kept her wonderful array of seasonings. She had basil, allspice, clove, dill, oregano, rosemary, savory, mace, nutmeg, stick cinnamon, and vanilla beans. She also had pickling lime, cream of tartar, peppercorns, cardamon, cumin, and a few others that I can't remember. Hanging on the wall she had a long plaited string of garlic, sprigs of thyme tied up in a bunch, a long string of dried red peppers, and next to it a few branches from her laurel tree, from which she made her bay leaves. Diagonally across from the wood stove was another stove that was used only when the weather began to get hot. This stove operated on kerosene. (We called it coal oil.) During the summer months, when the oil stove was used, it was my job (usually about every two weeks) to remove, clean, and trim the wicks, and put them back in the stove where they would operate very well for a time. The kitchen cabinet was called a "safe," and it contained such things as the flour, lard, sugar, rice, and potatoes.

On the wall opposite the fireplace were hung the pots, pans, skillets, and the bread bag which held the stale bread. In most Creole households, if space permitted, the icebox was placed out of the kitchen, or as far away from the heat as possible, since at best, it could only keep foods just a little cooler than the outside temperature.

But I started to tell you about Memere's **TURTLE STEW**, so now back to the recipe. For this stew you'll need:

4 lbs. turtle meat	4 bay leaves
4 tbsp. lard or oil	¼ tsp. ground cloves
4 tbsp. flour	¼ tsp. allspice
4 large onions, chopped	½ tsp. chili powder
3 cloves garlic, minced	1 tsp. basil
2 No. 2 cans tomatoes	½ tsp. powdered thyme
1 6-oz. can tomato paste	1 tsp. sugar
3 ribs celery, finely chopped	4 hard-cooked eggs
1 bell pepper, chopped	¼ lb. butter
½ cup dry sherry	1 lemon, sliced
¼ tsp. cayenne pepper	1 bunch green onions, finely
½ tsp. black pepper	chopped
salt to taste	

Don't let that formidable list of ingredients frighten you. This is not a difficult dish to prepare, and it is well worth the effort. First, boil the turtle meat for 5 minutes. In your heavy pot, heat the lard or oil and add the flour. When brown, add the onions, garlic, tomatoes, and tomato paste. Let this cook slowly for about 25 minutes and then add the turtle meat, which has been chopped into fairly large pieces. Add enough water to cover the meat, bring to a simmer, and let cook for ½ hour. While it is cooking, add the celery, bell pepper, sherry, and all the seasonings. After 30 minutes, mash the egg yolks and chop the whites; add to the stew and let cook slowly for 3 hours. If the stew gets too thick, just add a little more water. About ½ hour before serving, add the butter, lemon, and green onions. Correct the salt and pepper.

This is a marvelous stew served with rice or sometimes noodles or boiled spaghetti. Will serve six to eight.

STUFFED POCKET ROAST

7 to 10 lbs. shoulder roast,
   veal, or beef
2 tbsp. oil
1 lb. ground beef
½ lb. ground pork
2 cups chopped onions
1 cup chopped celery
1 bell pepper, chopped
3 cloves garlic, chopped
1 cup chopped green onions
   (shallots)

1 tsp. thyme
½ tsp. chili powder
¼ tsp. allspice
¼ tsp. cloves
2 tsp. salt
¼ tsp. cayenne
¼ tsp. black pepper
couple pinches of basil

Have your butcher debone the shoulder by removing the blade. Brown the ground beef and pork in the oil; pour off excess fat. Add onions, celery, bell pepper, garlic, and shallots. Cook until the vegetables are limp and a little transparent. Add seasonings. Fill the cavity of the roast with the ground meat mixture. When filled, either use a needle and thread to sew up the opening or use skewers, such as toothpicks.

Put the stuffed roast in a roasting pan. Sprinkle with a couple pinches of thyme, basil, garlic, and black pepper. In a preheated 325-degree oven, roast for 2½ to 3 hours.

Let the roast cool 15 minutes before slicing. Serve the stuffing surrounded by a border of solid meat.

ROAST POSSUM WITH STUFFING

I could not resist the temptation to include a recipe for roast possum with stuffing. To be sure, you will not find possum at your supermarket, but maybe a hunter in your family might bag one of the little critters. In that case, you will find this dish surprisingly tasty. You will need the following:

1 possum	**1 cup salt**
3 or 4 slices salt pork	
STUFFING:	

4 tbsp. butter	**½ bell pepper, chopped**
1 large onion, chopped	**2 cups crumbled cornbread**
2 stalks celery, chopped	**½ cup chopped pecans**

First, you have to dress the possum. Remove the head, tail, entrails, and skin. Also, remove the glands in the small of the back and under the front legs. Hang the possum outdoors for 2 days.

Wash the dressed possum thoroughly and place in a non-metallic bowl. Sprinkle 1 cup salt over it, cover with water, and let stand overnight. The next morning, drain and wash to remove the salt. Place in a large pot, cover with fresh water, and boil over medium heat for 5 minutes. Drain.

Fill a deep roasting pan with about 2 inches of water. Add the possum and cover the breast with strips of salt pork. Place the pan in a preheated 350-degree oven and bake for 1 hour, basting often with the juice in the bottom of the pan.

While the possum bakes, melt the butter in a frying pan and add the onions, celery, and green pepper. Cook until the vegetables are soft. Pour in the crumbled cornbread and add the pecans and sufficient liquid from the roasting pan to make a moist dressing. Take the possum from the oven and stuff it with the dressing. Return to the oven and roast for about 40 minutes, or until tender. Serve with baked sweet potatoes and mixed greens cooked with salt pork. Serves four.

BLANQUETTE d'AGNEAU

3 lbs. brisket of lamb
1 onion, finely chopped
2 carrots, finely sliced
6 shallots, finely chopped
½ stick butter
2 tbsp. flour
2 egg yolks
¼ lb. fresh mushrooms,
   sliced

2 bay leaves
⅛ tsp. powdered cloves
⅛ tsp. allspice
¼ tsp. thyme
1 pinch cayenne pepper
juice of 1 lemon
salt and pepper to taste

Cut the brisket into 2-inch square pieces. Put into a pot and cover with about ½ gallon of water. Add the onions, carrots, and a little salt and pepper and boil until the meat is tender. Drain, reserving the liquid.

In a heavy saucepan, melt the butter and sauté the shallots until tender. Mix in the flour and cook until nicely brown, stirring constantly. Add 1½ pints of the reserved liquid, the mushrooms, cloves, allspice, thyme, bay leaves, and cayenne and let the mixture simmer for about 20 minutes. Put the lamb back in the pot and simmer for 15 minutes more. Remove about ½ cup of the liquid and beat it into the 2 egg yolks and the lemon juice. Remove the pot from the heat, add the egg yolks, mix well, and serve.

This will serve four to six.

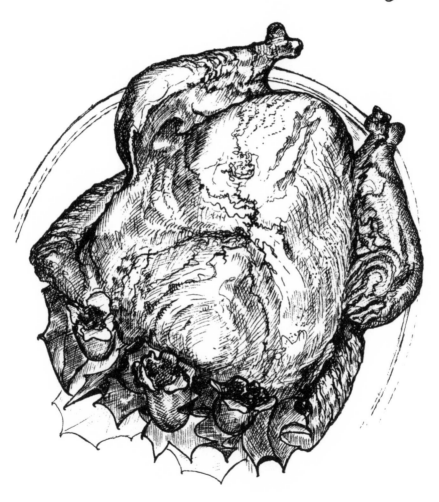

poultry

Pepere, my grandfather, was one of the most methodical of men. At a very early age I began to realize that I could predict with almost 100 percent accuracy what he would do from the time he arose in the morning until he retired at night. Would you believe he smoked one cigarette a day? He would have a smoke after breakfast and one in the afternoon.

His breakfast each morning consisted of two soft-boiled eggs. These had to be boiled to a state where the white was solid, but tender, and the yolk was liquid. I would sit at the breakfast table enthralled watching Pepere as he manipulated the eggs. After the eggs were boiled, they were brought to the table and placed in egg cups. Then with a teaspoon Pepere would crack around the top of the egg and remove a circular piece of the shell just about an inch in diameter. With his spoon he would remove some of the white and then dip slivers of buttered toast into the egg to absorb the fluid yolk.

When he was finished, he would remove a cigarette from his pack (he smoked a brand called "Coupons") and with a scissors would cut the cigarette in half. One half he put between his lips and lit, the other half he placed beside the clock on the mantel, and off to work he'd go.

Pepere was not one to work long hours during the regular work week. He was a "crier" in Judge Skinner's court, and was usually home about the time we were returning from school. He would first change his clothes, and then wind and set the clock. Memere had a large mantel clock that chimed the half hour and the hour. The only one allowed to touch it was Pepere. He would open the case, take the key, and wind and set the clock. He then took his half of a cigarette, brought it to the table, and before he lit it he would have his afternoon snack. Invariably the snack was half an apple and half a glass of claret wine. Memere would core the apple half and Pepere, with a spoon, would scrape the inside until nothing was left but a very thin skin. When the apple was finished he would take a couple of slices of French bread, break the bread into bite-size pieces, and dip them in the wine. He dunked until the wine glass was dry, and then lit his half cigarette. Then Pepere got up from the table, for it was time for his walk to the corner.

At the corner of Elysian Fields and Urquhart streets stood a shoemaker's shop. Pepere visited the shop each afternoon. I liked to go with him just to watch the men as they repaired the shoes. The workers in the shop spoke only Italian, and Pepere gradually got to the point where he could converse in simple Italian. He would spend about an hour in the shop and then retrace his steps toward home.

One of Pepere's favorites (and so Memere cooked it often) was **BUTTERMILK CHICKEN**. For the dish Memere would assemble:

1 fryer, cut in pieces	½ tsp. salt
1 tbsp. lard or oil	⅛ tsp. black pepper
2 tbsp. butter	dash of pepper sauce
1 medium onion, chopped fine	½ cup finely chopped green onions
1 1-lb. can whole tomatoes, drained	¼ cup parsley
1¼ cups buttermilk	1½ tsp. dill weed
¼ tsp. sugar	¼ tsp. lemon juice
	1 cup sour cream

First, she put the butter and lard or oil into the pot; when it was hot, she would add the chicken pieces. These would be cooked until brown. Next, the onion was added and sautéed until soft (about 5 minutes) over a low fire. Into the pot went the tomatoes, buttermilk, sugar, salt, pepper, and pepper sauce. The mixture was allowed to simmer for about 25 minutes. After 25 minutes the green onions, parsley, and dill were added, and the mixture was cooked, uncovered, for 5 minutes longer. The lemon juice and the sour cream were stirred in and heated.

Served with some French bread and a glass of rosé, it was a treat! Serves four.

CHICKEN CREOLE

3½ lbs. frying chicken
¼ cup olive oil
1 16-oz. can tomatoes
1 tsp. salt
few grains pepper
few grains cayenne
½ tsp. powdered thyme
1 tbsp. minced parsley
2 bay leaves

3 cloves garlic, minced
2 tbsp. flour
6 shallots, chopped
½ cup minced onion
½ cup chopped green
  pepper
½ cup dry white wine
2 10½-oz. cans beef
  consommé

Cut the chicken into pieces; wipe pieces with clean damp cloth. Sauté in olive oil, turning to brown both sides. Remove the chicken and add to the pot the onion, shallots, and green pepper; sauté slowly for 5 minutes. Add the flour and stir constantly over a low heat for another 5 minutes. Add the tomatoes, garlic, parsley, bay leaves, thyme, pepper, salt, wine, and consommé. Let this simmer for 10 minutes, then add the chicken. Cover and slowly simmer for about 45 minutes or until the chicken is tender.

Serve over hot cooked rice garnished with avocado slices and parsley sprigs. Serves four to six.

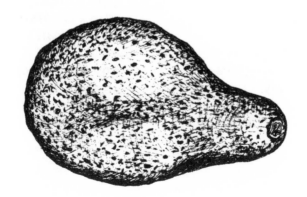

CHICKEN FRICASSÉE

1 large chicken, cut in
  pieces
2 large onions, chopped
1 large bell pepper,
  chopped
1 cup chopped celery
½ cup oil
flour
½ tsp. thyme

2 bay leaves
¼ tsp. cayenne pepper
1 tbsp. minced parsley
½ cup finely chopped
  shallots
salt and pepper to taste
1½ qts. water or chicken
  stock

Dredge the chicken in flour and brown in the oil. Remove the chicken and add the onions, bell pepper, and celery to the oil; sauté slowly for 5 minutes. Add 1½ quarts of water or stock along with the bay leaves, thyme, salt, pepper, and cayenne. Put the chicken back in the pot and slowly simmer, covered, until the chicken is tender.

About 5 minutes before the chicken is done, add the chopped shallots and parsley. This is good served over rice. Serves four to six.

CHICKEN JAMBALAYA

1 4 to 5 lb. hen, cut up
½ cup lard or other
  shortening
3 onions, chopped
1 small can tomatoes
5 stalks celery, chopped
3 cups long grain rice
salt and pepper to taste

1½ qts. chicken stock or 3
  cans consommé and
  enough water to make 1½
  qts.
½ cup finely chopped green
  onions
½ cup minced parsley
½ tsp. Tabasco

Salt and pepper the chicken pieces. Fry in the shortening in a heavy saucepan until brown. Remove the chicken and fry the onions and celery for 5 minutes. Mix in the tomatoes and Tabasco. Fry for a couple of minutes, then replace the chicken and add the stock. Cook at a simmer until the chicken is tender.

Add the salt, pepper, and the rice. Turn the heat very low and cook until the rice is tender. Add the green onions and parsley, mix well, and let stand for 5 minutes before serving. Serves six to eight.

CHICKEN A LA LOUISIANE

1 chicken, boiled until tender	12 mushrooms, sliced
1 tbsp. oil	6 olives, pitted
6 tbsp. butter	4 artichoke hearts
1 tbsp. flour	¼ cup sherry
1 10½-oz. can beef consommé	salt and cayenne pepper to taste

Disjoint the chicken, cut into pieces, and fry in the oil and 4 tablespoons butter until brown. Set aside on a platter in a warm oven.

Melt the remaining 2 tablespoons butter in a heavy frying pan. Add the flour, cook over a very low heat 5 minutes, and add the consommé. Mix well and cook to a creamy thickness, stirring constantly. Add the mushrooms, olives, artichoke hearts, sherry, and salt and cayenne pepper to taste. Cook a few minutes longer, then pour the sauce over the chicken. Serves four.

CHICKEN MAQUECHOUX CREOLE

2 tbsp. oil
3 tbsp. butter
2 fryers, cut up
4½ cups fresh corn kernels, scraped off the cob
1 cup beef consommé
3 tbsp. heavy cream
4 onions, chopped

1 bell pepper, chopped
3 fresh tomatoes, coarsely chopped
⅛ tsp. powdered allspice
¼ tsp. powdered thyme
½ tsp. basil
2 shakes Tabasco
1 tbsp. minced parsley

In a heavy pot heat the oil and butter over a medium heat. Brown the chicken parts, turning them frequently to get an even brown. Turn the heat low and add the corn, consommé, and cream. Mix thoroughly and then add the onion, bell pepper, tomatoes, and the rest of the ingredients. Cook over a very low heat for a good 40 minutes or until the chicken is tender, stirring frequently.

Serve over hot rice. This should serve six to eight.

Memere used to say, "on devient cuisiner, mais on née rotisseur," which, freely translated, meant "one could be taught to cook but one is born a roaster."

Now, this may not be altogether true, but doubt it not, roasting is an art. Of course with today's ovens, most of the guesswork is removed, and successfully roasting a fat hen is a rather simple task if—and it is a big "IF"—certain well-established procedures are followed.

In the first place, roasting is not baking, even though both are done inside the oven. In roasting, the meat is cooked quickly, with the outside to a golden brown to hold in the juices. When you cut into well-roasted meat, it is tender and wonderfully juicy. So how do you do it? As Toulouse Lautrec explains in his recipe for rabbit stew, first you catch a rabbit!

So, first you get a chicken. What *kind* of chicken is very important if you really want to wind up enjoying a beautifully roasted bird. Please do *not* go to the nearest supermarket and pick up a fryer or two and expect to do a good job. What you need is a roasting hen.

What's a roasting hen? Let's start at the beginning. Among killed and drawn poultry in the markets, the broilers are the youngest, averaging about eight and a half to ten weeks in age. Then come the fryers, which go up to about three months. Following the fryers we have the roasting hens; they can go up to nine months old. Bear in mind that while the younger chickens are the most tender, they lack the flavor of the older ones, so that in the roasting hen, the optimum tenderness and flavor are reached. Those older than the roasters become the stewing chickens, which have to be cooked for hours before they are tender. So, let's get a roasting chicken.

If you really want to capture the true roasting flavor, find a market where you can purchase a hen "on the hoof," have it killed and drawn, bring it home, and cook it while it's still warm. You will need about a 4 pound roasting chicken. I might tell you at this point that there are two schools of thought as to what temperature should be utilized. One school says 325° throughout, the other says sear the chicken at a high temperature and reduce the heat as the meat cooks. I think the latter method will give better results, but either way, if you pursue the following directions, you can't miss.

Take the bird in hand and with a damp cloth, wipe (do not wash) inside and out. Rub the cavity with some salt and black pepper and a couple of pinches of powdered thyme. Now, place the bird on a wire rack in a shallow roasting pan. Tie the wings and legs together, so it will look better as it is taken to the table after cooking. Rub softened butter (not margarine) all over the chicken, then sprinkle with salt and pepper. In the pan place a chopped onion, a chopped bell pepper, a bay leaf, and a pinch of thyme. Throw in a couple of cups of water. The vegetables will flavor the drippings as the chicken cooks.

The oven should be heated to 475°. Place the chicken in the oven and cook for about 15 minutes. Baste two or three times during the 15 minutes with the liquid in the bottom of the pan. At about this time, the bird should be a nice brown. Place a piece of aluminum foil loosely over the chicken (just enough to cover the drumsticks and the breast), basting the while until the chicken is done. One way of testing is to look at the juices inside the cavity. They should be clear with no traces of pink. Another way is to stick the thickest part of the thigh with a fork. If the juices run out clear, the chicken is done. When done, remove the chicken to a serving dish and keep it warm.

Now for the gravy. Take ½ pound of fresh mushrooms and brown in a little butter seasoned with a little salt and pepper. Add the mushrooms to the juices in the roasting pan. Pour in 1 cup of heavy cream and heat on top of the stove, stirring and scraping. This must not boil, but barely simmer. After 10 minutes of simmering, the gravy is ready.

In carving your roasted fowl, wait at least 15 minutes so that the juice will be able to redistribute itself in the meat. Spoon the gravy over each piece as it is served. Will serve four to six.

ROAST CHICKEN

1 4-lb. roasting chicken	1 onion, chopped
salt	1 bell pepper, chopped
black pepper	1 bay leaf
a few pinches of powdered	½ lb. fresh mushrooms
thyme	1 cup heavy cream
butter	

CHICKEN SAUCE PIQUANTE

8 chicken thighs
1½ cups finely chopped
  onions
1 cup finely chopped celery
1 cup finely chopped bell
  pepper
1 cup chopped shallots
1 tbsp. finely chopped
  parsley
1 16-oz. can tomatoes
2 tbsp. butter
¼ cup oil
4 tbsp. flour
1 6-oz. can tomato paste

4 cloves garlic, finely
  chopped
2 10¾-oz. cans chicken
  consommé
2 cans water
1 lemon, thinly sliced
¼ tsp. cayenne pepper
¼ tsp. black pepper
1½ tsp. salt
1 tsp. chili powder
1 tsp. basil
½ tsp. thyme
4 bay leaves

Brown the chicken in a heavy Dutch oven in ¼ cup of oil; remove and set aside. Pour out all but about 2 tablespoons oil, add 2 tablespoons butter, and when hot add the onions, celery, and bell pepper. Sauté slowly until the vegetables begin to change color and become transparent. Sprinkle in the flour and mix well over a low fire, stirring for about 5 minutes. Add the tomatoes and tomato paste and cook 5 minutes longer. Pour in the consommé and water, stirring and mixing well. As this simmers slowly, add the garlic, lemon, cayenne pepper, black pepper, salt, basil, thyme, chili powder, and bay leaves. Let this simmer for about ½ hour and then add the chicken thighs. Cook until the chicken is tender. A few minutes before the chicken is done, add the shallots and parsley.

When the chicken is done, remove from the fire and let set for ½ hour. At this time the seasoning can be corrected. (More salt may be added.) Serve over hot white rice. Serves four to six.

CHICKEN SAUSAGE JAMBALAYA

5 cups chicken stock (or dissolved chicken bouillon cubes or consommé)

First, place the chicken trimmings (such as the neck, wing ends, fat, and skin) into a pot of cold water, and then add 2 bay leaves and a good handful of green onion tops. (Don't use the chicken liver.) Bring to a boil and cook slowly for 2 hours.

1 lb. andouille sausage, sliced into ¼-inch lengths
2 chickens (fryers), cut up
2 to 2½ cups white onions (5 small), finely chopped
1 medium green pepper, finely chopped
4 stalks celery, finely chopped
3 tbsp. cooking oil
4 tbsp. flour
½ 6-oz. can tomato paste
1 10½-oz. can beef consommé
2 bay leaves
1 tsp. basil leaves
½ tsp. chili powder
¼ tsp. red pepper
black pepper (sprinkle light)
1 tsp. salt
3 small cloves garlic, finely chopped
2½ cups raw rice (Uncle Ben's Converted Rice)
6 green onions with tops, finely chopped
parsley (small handful), chopped
dash Tabasco

Pour the cooking oil into a heavy iron pot and heat. Add andouille sausage and brown very well over medium heat. Remove sausage and set aside. Place the chicken into the pot and brown very well, turning as needed. After the chicken has browned, remove and set aside. Add a small amount of cooking oil if needed and the flour; make a medium brown roux. Add chopped vegetables (except green onions and parsley) and cook until tender, stirring as needed. Add ½ can tomato paste and stir well into mixture as cooking continues. Add 1 can beef consommé and gradually add 3 to 4 cans stock as mixture is stirred. Bring to a slow boil, and then add sausage and chicken, stirring well. Let boiling resume, then add seasonings and the chopped garlic. Cover and cook at a slow boil for 15 minutes, stirring occasionally. Add 2½ cups rice and stir well. Bring back to a very slow boil, cover, and cook for 25 to 30 minutes without uncovering. Add chopped green onions and parsley and stir well. Add a dash of Tabasco and stir. Remove from heat, let set for 5 minutes, then serve.

Ham and shrimp also make an excellent Jambalaya. Prepare as above. Oysters may be added to Jambalaya if desired. Add after the other cooking is complete. Cook oysters about 3 minutes (until the edges begin to curl). Serve immediately. Serves six to eight.

CHICKEN AND SOUR CREAM

1 fryer, cut up
1 cup finely chopped
  shallots
½ lb. fresh mushrooms,
  sliced
1 8-oz. carton of sour cream
½ cup dry white wine (such
  as Chablis or vermouth)

1 stick butter
1 tbsp. oil
⅛ tsp. cayenne pepper
1 cup water or chicken
  stock
salt and pepper to taste

Salt and pepper the chicken pieces and brown them in a heavy skillet in the butter and oil. Remove the chicken, add the green onions and mushrooms, and sauté for 5 minutes over a very low fire. Add the sour cream, stock, cayenne, salt, black pepper, and chicken. Cover and simmer slowly until chicken is tender, about 20 to 25 minutes. Add the wine and stir well, then cook for 5 more minutes. Serve over rice. Will serve four.

POULET BLANC

3 chicken breasts (six half
breasts), deboned
3 tbsp. olive oil
3 toes of garlic, finely
chopped
2 tbsp. lemon juice
½ tsp. thyme
½ tsp. salt

1 stick butter
1 tbsp. oil
4 shallots, finely chopped
5 tbsp. flour
3 cups whole milk
black pepper
2 dashes Tabasco
pinch of ground nutmeg

The chicken breasts have to be deboned, and this is not as formidable a task as it is thought to be. Hold the breast with the inside (or bone side) facing you and with the pointed end toward the left. Fold in half, away from you, and the bone will crack in half. Now, keep shoving the thumbs between the meat and the bones, and in a short time, and with a little practice, you'll be able to debone chicken breasts without a knife, in less than half a minute.

Place the deboned breast between two pieces of wax paper and with the flat of your cleaver, pound the meat hard until it spreads almost double. Slice the flattened breasts into strips. Marinate for one hour in the olive oil, garlic, lemon juice, thyme, and salt. Stir a few times.

After the meat has been marinated, melt the butter in your heavy skillet, add the oil, and fry the strips of chicken for 2 minutes on each side. (Do not overcook, as chicken breasts have a tendency to get a little rubbery if cooked too long.) Remove the chicken and add the shallots to the pan; sauté until tender. Add the flour, mix well, and, stirring constantly, cook for 4 minutes. Add the milk slowly, stirring all the while and mixing well. Salt and pepper to taste and add the two dashes of Tabasco. When the milk begins to simmer, return the chicken to the pan and allow to simmer slowly for a few minutes until the sauce is thickened and the chicken is heated.

Add the nutmeg, stir, and the dish is ready to serve. It can be served over noodles or a slice of toast. Serves four to six.

POULET A LA BONNE FEMME

2 fryers, or equivalent
  weight in chicken breasts
  or thighs
10 medium-sized potatoes
1 lb. bacon
4 large onions, thinly sliced
poultry seasoning (This is
  the name of a particular
  type seasoning.)

½ cup chopped shallots
salt and black pepper to
  taste
2 tbsp. chopped parsley

In your old iron pot slowly fry the bacon until crisp and then remove it. Cut the chicken in pieces, season with salt and pepper, and fry until brown in the bacon grease; reserve. Peel the potatoes and slice each lengthwise into three slices (no thinner); brown in the bacon drippings and remove. If there is anymore than about 4 tablespoons of grease, remove the surplus.

In your pot put a layer of chicken, over it a layer of potatoes, then a layer of thinly sliced onion, and top with a layer of thin bacon. Sprinkle a couple of pinches of poultry seasoning and then repeat with a layer of chicken, potatoes, onions, and bacon. Sprinkle a little more poultry seasoning and add a few pinches of salt and pepper. Top this with the chopped shallots and parsley.

Preheat the oven to 350°, cover your pot, and let it bake for 40 minutes, then uncovered for 15 more minutes. This, along with French bread and green salad, will serve six adults.

CREAMED ROCK CORNISH HEN

6 hens
enough chicken broth to
cover hens
6 chicken bouillon cubes
1 large onion, finely
chopped
4 bay leaves
½ tbsp. powdered thyme
¼ tsp. pepper sauce

¼ tsp. black pepper
4 ribs celery, chopped
3 cups cooked rice
12 strips bacon
6 green onions, minced
½ tsp. poultry seasoning
garlic salt and pepper to
taste
1 stick butter

SAUCE:

6 tbsp. butter
6 tbsp. flour
1 bunch green onions,
minced
4 tbsp. dry white wine

4 cups milk
½ cup grated Parmesan
cheese
⅛ tsp. grated nutmeg
salt and pepper to taste

Use a pot large enough to hold the six hens. Put the chicken broth in, add the bouillon cubes, onions, bay leaves, thyme, pepper sauce, black pepper, and celery, and bring to a boil. While boiling, place the birds in the pot. When the liquid begins to boil again, let it cook for 5 minutes. Turn the heat off and cover; allow the hens to remain in the hot liquid for 10 minutes, then remove and drain. Reserve the liquid for a soup.

Fry the bacon in a large skillet until crisp; remove and reserve. Cook the birds in the bacon grease, turning frequently until they are brown. Place the cooked rice in a bowl. Chop the bacon very finely and add to the rice. Add the minced green onions, along with the poultry seasoning and the salt and pepper, and mix well. Stuff the birds with the mixture, tie the legs together, and place in a well-greased pan. Brush each hen with melted butter, place in a preheated 370-degree oven, and bake for ½ hour. Remove from oven, put the hens on a platter, and pour the sauce over them.

To make the sauce, first melt the butter in a large skillet or saucepan.

CREAMED ROCK CORNISH HEN

6 hens
enough chicken broth to
   cover hens
6 chicken bouillon cubes
1 large onion, finely
   chopped
4 bay leaves
½ tbsp. powdered thyme
¼ tsp. pepper sauce

¼ tsp. black pepper
4 ribs celery, chopped
3 cups cooked rice
12 strips bacon
6 green onions, minced
½ tsp. poultry seasoning
garlic salt and pepper to
   taste
1 stick butter

SAUCE:

6 tbsp. butter
6 tbsp. flour
1 bunch green onions,
   minced
4 tbsp. dry white wine

4 cups milk
½ cup grated Parmesan
   cheese
⅛ tsp. grated nutmeg
salt and pepper to taste

Use a pot large enough to hold the six hens. Put the chicken broth in, add the bouillon cubes, onions, bay leaves, thyme, pepper sauce, black pepper, and celery, and bring to a boil. While boiling, place the birds in the pot. When the liquid begins to boil again, let it cook for 5 minutes. Turn the heat off and cover; allow the hens to remain in the hot liquid for 10 minutes, then remove and drain. Reserve the liquid for a soup.

Fry the bacon in a large skillet until crisp; remove and reserve. Cook the birds in the bacon grease, turning frequently until they are brown. Place the cooked rice in a bowl. Chop the bacon very finely and add to the rice. Add the minced green onions, along with the poultry seasoning and the salt and pepper, and mix well. Stuff the birds with the mixture, tie the legs together, and place in a well-greased pan. Brush each hen with melted butter, place in a preheated 370-degree oven, and bake for ½ hour. Remove from oven, put the hens on a platter, and pour the sauce over them.

To make the sauce, first melt the butter in a large skillet or saucepan.

bread under the broiler until the cheese is melted. Place a slice on each plate. Pour the chicken and sauce over each slice, then top with the grated cheddar cheese. Run the plates under the broiler again until the cheese melts. Serve immediately. Will serve six to eight.

POULET SAUTÉ PARISIAN

6 chicken breasts	salt and pepper to taste
1 stick butter	1 shake Tabasco
2 tomatoes, peeled and chopped	pinch of paprika
	4 scallions, minced
1 cup dry white wine	½ tsp. dried tarragon
¼ cup heavy cream	1 tsp. Kitchen Bouquet
2 cloves garlic, minced	2 tbsp. brandy

Season the chicken with salt and pepper. In a heavy pot melt the butter and slowly sauté the chicken until brown. Add the brandy, mix well, and then add the tomatoes, scallions, garlic, Tabasco, paprika, wine, and tarragon. Let the mixture slowly simmer until chicken is tender. Stir in the cream and Kitchen Bouquet. Serve with brabant potatoes. Will serve four to six.

Those were the wonderful days—as children we lived them in a constant state of feverish anticipation—those days close to Thanksgiving, Christmas, and New Year's. It was hard to fall asleep at night just thinking about what was coming, and the daylight hours dragged and dragged. The first of the holidays was Thanksgiving, and all we could think about was food and goodies.

Of course, we knew Christmas meant surprises and presents and the New Year's meant another marvelous meal, a change of the calendar, and a time for scribbling out a few new "I resolve to's. . . . "

Those holiday meals took a great deal more advance preparation than anything you would whip up nowadays. Of course, the turkey was king, but choosing it involved more than just a casual trip to the market to make a selection in the frozen food section. Our turkeys were bought "on the hoof"! On the day we decided to buy our turkey, the whole family went to the market. This was usually about three weeks before the holiday.

At the French Market, we would go from cage to cage until we found a likely prospect for our dinner. Then the poultry man was requested to remove the bird from the cage for inspection. Memere and Mamete would both have to agree before the turkey was finally chosen. The bird was examined from beak to toenail. It was felt all over to determine its plumpness or lack thereof. The end of the breast-bone was wiggled to be sure we weren't buying a "grandfather Tom," and after due deliberation and consultation, the bird was bought and carted off for home.

At home he was immediately put in a cage to be fattened even further. A pan of corn was left in the cage at all times so that Mr. Turkey could eat to his heart's content. With a little water to wash it down, what more could a turkey ask for?

But soon the day would arrive when the supreme sacrifice had to be made, when the turkey was killed, plucked, and eviscerated (we called it gutted). All this was done the day before the roasting, giving Memere time to marinate the turkey and allowing time for the seasonings to spread their marvelous flavors through the meat.

First, Memere would mix together a cup of olive oil, 4 tablespoons lemon juice, 4 tablespoons Worcestershire sauce, 6 cloves garlic, minced, 1 bunch green onions, minced, ½ teaspoon powdered thyme, ¼ teaspoon cayenne pepper, 1 teaspoon salt, and ¼ teaspoon black pepper. The next step was interesting and not as difficult as it may seem at first. She would start at the back of the turkey and with her fingers would separate the skin from the meat. Then she would shove her fingers under the skin. Soon most of the skin was separated from the meat, even the skin on the drumsticks. She would work the marinade in under the skin (again with her fingers) until it was almost gone. (She would save a little for the outside.) When the outside was coated, the turkey was covered with brown paper or put into a paper bag and put into the icebox overnight.

Of course, the turkey situation has undergone radical changes through the years, necessitating different procedures in buying and

POULTRY · 167

roasting your bird, so what follows is probably more appropriate to producing today's holiday dinner.

First, I'll explain the method of selecting the proper **TURKEY**. Regarding the size, remember that with a turkey under 12 pounds you'll need ¾ to 1 pound per person. For turkeys over 12 pounds figure ½ to ¾ pounds per serving. For economy's sake, do not buy birds under 10 pounds, because the ratio of meat to weight is much less than the larger birds. Should you get a hen or tom? Years ago hens were considered better than toms (more tender), but with today's feeding methods and modern turkey breeding there is now very little difference. Actually, if you want a very large turkey (18 to 30 pounds) you'll have to get a tom. Look for grade "A," and if you don't see the stamp ask your butcher or store manager what grade you are buying. Turkeys are graded according to quality—A, B, C, with grade A being the best.

Should you buy a fresh or frozen turkey? Surprisingly, frozen turkeys are, for the most part, fresher than the non-frozen ones. Frozen turkeys are flash-frozen immediately after they are killed, whereas the unfrozen bird may be kept in cold storage for a couple of weeks. Defrosting is a very important operation to retain the turkey's flavor. First, leave the turkey in the plastic bag. Set it in a large pan and put in the *refrigerator*, not outside on the counter or drainboard, and defrost it *slowly*. If the turkey weighs around 13 pounds, let it thaw for 4 days. If around 16 pounds plan on 5 days. This may mean a little more work, but it's well worth it. Of course, if you have to defrost quickly, fill the sink with water and put the turkey in the water, leaving it in the plastic bag, changing the water several times.

After the turkey has been thawed, the next step is to marinate the bird. Earlier we told you how Memere marinated her turkey. Follow her recipe. The turkey should be marinated at least one day before it is roasted. (Two days would be even better.) Put the turkey in a plastic bag and leave in the refrigerator until ready to roast.

Now for the stuffing. For the **OYSTER STUFFING** you need:

½ cup minced onions
1½ cups chopped celery
½ cup chopped shallots
½ stick butter
4 cups cooked rice
2 tbsp. chopped parsley
1 tbsp. poultry seasoning
½ tsp. powdered thyme

¼ tsp. cayenne pepper
1½ tsp. salt
1 tsp. black pepper
2 doz. oysters, chopped,
  and their liquid
1 cup stock or chicken
  broth
2 eggs, slightly beaten

Your stuffing will be so much better if you get freshly shucked oysters rather than bottled or canned. So try to find a seafood store where you can get fresh oysters. First of all, sauté the onions, shallots, and celery in butter. When the vegetables are softened (after about 4 to 5 minutes), add the rice, parsley, seasonings, oysters, and stock. Mix very well and heat, stirring, over a low fire for about 5 minutes. Remove from the fire, add the beaten eggs, and mix well. This makes enough for about a 10-pound turkey.

The **CORNBREAD DRESSING** *was always my favorite, and here, for my taste, is one of the best recipes. You will need:*

6 cups crumbled cornbread
4 cups bread crumbs
3 cups milk
2 onions, chopped
½ cup chopped shallots
1 cup chopped celery
6 tbsp. butter
4 eggs, well beaten
1 tsp. basil

2 tsp. salt
1 tsp. black pepper
1 tsp. poultry seasoning
1 qt. beef stock
⅛ tsp. powdered cloves
⅛ tsp. powdered allspice
½ tsp. thyme
½ tsp. garlic powder

Soak the cornbread and bread crumbs in the milk. Sauté the onions, shallots, and celery in the butter until the vegetables are soft. Combine the cornbread and crumbs with the sautéed vegetables, and after mixing, add the eggs. Mix well, then stir in the seasonings and stock. You can stuff a 12-pound turkey with this.

You should only stuff your bird about three-quarters full because the stuffing will swell. I might also warn you not to leave a stuffed bird sitting out all day on the table, since stuffing spoils much quicker than the turkey. Some prefer to cook the stuffing separately to eliminate the danger of spoilage. In that case, the mixture can be put in a dish and baked, covered, for 1 hour at 325°.

Roast the turkey in a brown paper bag. For a turkey over 15 pounds preheat the oven to 300°, under 15 pounds, 325°. You should allow about 20 minutes per pound for a stuffed turkey and about 15 minutes per pound if the bird is unstuffed. Get a double strength grocery bag and place the seam side up. I must warn you that a turkey should not be roasted in a recycled paper bag, so be sure the bag you use is not made of recycled paper. (The bags are usually stamped if they are recycled.)

Take about 1 stick of butter or margarine and spread it on the bottom of the bag. Slip the turkey into the bag neck first with the breast down. Secure the end of the bag with a string or paper clips. Set the bag on a rack over a shallow pan and put into the oven. Do not open the oven door until 30 minutes before a 10- to 16-pound turkey would be done or 1 hour before a 17- to 25-pound turkey would be done.

Take the pan out of the oven and make a small hole in the bag just under the breast. Let all the juice run into the pan, then empty the pan into a bowl and save for a gravy. Now take the bag off. Turn the turkey around, breast side up, put back on the rack and pan, and return to the oven. Baste a few times with any leftover marinade and cook for ½ hour longer for the small turkeys and 1 hour for the large turkeys. To test the turkey for doneness, stick a fork into the thick part of the leg. If the juice comes out clear, the turkey is done. Another way to test is to wiggle a drumstick. If it wiggles easily, the turkey is ready. Remove the turkey from the oven and place a piece of foil over it just to retain a little of the heat. Before carving, let it stand for about 15 minutes. This firms up the meat, improves the flavor, and makes carving much easier.

One of the dishes Memere loved to cook was "Salmi de Poules d'Eau aux Navets," or as we might translate that today, "Stewed Poule d'Eau with turnips." Poules d'Eau was pronounced "Pull doo," and I'm firmly convinced that the only reason Memere delighted in cooking the aforementioned dish was because it was such a challenge.

You see, most cooks would never have bothered with cooking a Poules d'Eau. Unless you really knew how to go about it, it could be a vile tasting mess. I'll explain how she cooked the bird a little later, but for now, let me tell you a few interesting facts about how the Creoles treated the Poules d'Eau. The bird is a species of water duck resembling both a chicken and a duck, hence the name "water chicken." Forty or fifty years ago, before the Lakefront was filled and developed, close to Lake Pontchartrain where it met the Industrial Canal were marsh lands. In these marshes at certain times of the year could be found literally thousands of these "marsh hens" as they were also called. Any hunter could walk the L & N tracks to the Industrial Canal and in a matter of minutes end up with a basketful of Poules d'Eau. There being no bag limit, the birds were slaughtered indiscriminately.

Since the bird lived entirely in the water and marshes and never came to dry land, it was designated by the Creoles as a fish, and could be served as a Friday or Fast Day fish. Of course, since the Poules d'Eau fed mostly on fish, its meat had a disagreeable fish taste and in the hands of an inexperienced cook was most unpalatable.

Here is the way Memere used to get rid of the fish taste or any other objectionable wild taste in any game she cooked. First, she filled a kettle with water and boiled it. Then she added a chopped onion or two and a couple of peeled, chopped turnips. She would cook the Poules d'Eau in the water until the odor was gone. (This usually took only a few minutes.) Voila! The bird was now ready to be stewed into a delectable dish. However, since Poules d'Eau have become a scarce commodity, instead let me pass on to you lovers of wild birds a delightful way of cooking **WILD DUCK**.

Take a pair of ducks, clean them well, and cut into pieces at the joints. Put 1 tablespoon of butter and 2 onions, finely chopped, into a Dutch oven. Let this brown and then add the pieces of duck. When the ducks are brown, add ½ cup minced ham, 6 turnips cut into quarters, and 1 teaspoon flour. Stir well and let the flour brown slightly.

POULTRY · 171

Now add ¼ teaspoon thyme, 2 tablespoons chopped parsley, 2 bay leaves, and 3 cloves of garlic, finely chopped. Stir well and let the whole mixture smother for about 15 minutes, stirring frequently so it won't burn. Add enough water to cover the ducks and stir well. Cover tightly and let the mixture smother on a low fire another ½ hour, then season to taste with salt and black pepper.

This is one of the nicest duck dishes the Creoles ever concocted! Serves four to six.

2 wild ducks
1 tbsp. butter
2 onions, finely chopped
½ cup minced ham
6 turnips, cut into quarters
1 tsp. flour
¼ tsp. thyme

2 tbsp. chopped parsley
2 bay leaves
3 cloves garlic, finely
** chopped**
salt and black pepper to
** taste**

egg
dishes

Whenever I get to reminiscing or waxing nostalgic (some call it the first sign of old age, or living in the past, or even the first sign of senility), I become mindful of the changes the past 50 years have wrought in the structure of the family. Today's grandparents are looked upon by most of the younger generation as—what shall I say—old fogies? Now, in my youth (there I go again), the grandparents occupied a much stronger position in the hierarchy. For example, I can recall very vividly that Memere was almost the supreme authority when it came to the family's health.

Whenever any sickness developed, it was Memere who was called, even before the doctor. (In the old days, doctors made house calls.) Actually, she decided whether she was going to treat the patient or whether the privilege should be delegated to a doctor. If she decided she would handle the case, the services of the M.D. were dispensed with. Those old Creoles had a remedy for every possible ailment. Some of them were very effective, although there were others that had no basis in any scientific fact, and were, for the most part, worthless.

I can recall that whenever we had a bad chest cold, Memere's remedy was olive oil and turpentine. The formula was made of equal parts of oil (we called it sweet oil) and turpentine. About ½ cup of the mixture was put in a pie pan and warmed over the heater. This concoction was then rubbed on the patient's chest, after which a piece of flannel was used to cover the rubbed part. You slept with your chest covered with the flannel. Would you believe it, it worked! In later years, I was informed by one of the medical profession that the aforementioned mixture was as good as any of the patent rubs.

Mamete's remedy for colds was, first of all, to take a couple of white onions, slice them thinly, and put them in a bowl. Then she sprinkled 3 or 4 tablespoons of sugar over the onion and let it stand overnight. Somehow, the sugar and onions combined to make a syrup which proved to be an effective cold fighter.

When the illness was cured and the patient was on the mend, he, like all convalescents, had to have beef tea. This was made with a pound or two of beef stew. The meat was put into a wide-mouthed bottle. Then the bottle was covered, put in a pot of water, and the heat was turned on. The bottle was left in the boiling water for 3 hours. The meat in the bottle (I guess because of the heat) produced a cup or two of pure meat juice which, with a little salt, was delicious.

Of course, one of the treats for having overcome your disease was to be able to eat those luscious **EGG CUSTARDS**. They were very simple to make. All you had to do was to combine ½ cup sugar and the juice of ½ lemon in a skillet, stirring over low heat until the sugar was melted and turned into a caramel-colored liquid. Pour this into a 9-inch x 5-inch x 3-inch baking dish. (Cover the entire bottom with the liquid.) Beat 8 egg yolks, 5 whole eggs, and 1¼ cups sugar together, then beat in 4½ cups hot milk and 1 teaspoon vanilla. Pour this mixture into the dish with the caramel.

Place the baking dish in a pan of hot water in a 350-degree oven for about an hour, or until the custard is just firm. Cool, then chill.

Before serving, turn custard out of the baking dish by first loosening the edges with a sharp knife and then inverting on a serving dish. This will serve eight to ten.

1¾ cups sugar	5 eggs
juice of ½ lemon	4½ cups hot milk
8 egg yolks	1 tsp. vanilla

SCRAMBLED EGGS

a few tbsp. sweet butter	2 or 3 eggs
2 tbsp. sour cream	

Melt the butter in a warm heavy frying pan. Add the sour cream, then break the eggs into the pan. Mix slowly with a spoon (do not beat), and let the eggs warm with the pan, gradually pulling in the sides as the eggs cook. The eggs are done when they are lightly blended and set.

Herbs or grated cheese may be added halfway through the process. This particular recipe should take about ½ hour to prepare.

A basic omelet is made with 3 eggs. Never attempt to make an omelet using more than 5 eggs at one time. The omelet pan should be heavy, carefully seasoned, and must be very hot. Omelets should never be cooked more than 1 minute, and should never be allowed to brown.

PLAIN THREE EGG OMELET

3 eggs
3 tsp. cold water
2 drops Tabasco

salt and black pepper to
taste
1 tbsp. butter

Break the eggs into a small mixing bowl. Add the water, Tabasco, and salt and black pepper. Melt the butter in an omelet pan. (Do not allow to burn.) Beat the eggs 40 to 50 strokes with a fork, then pour into the melted butter in the omelet pan. Stir with a fork, working the cooked egg toward the center of the pan. Do not cook more than 1 minute.

Carefully slide the omelet from the pan onto the plate, folding over as it slides from the pan. The omelet will continue cooking after it is removed from the pan.

GREEN ONION OMELET

3 eggs
3 tsp. cold water
2 drops Tabasco
salt and black pepper to
taste

1 tbsp. butter (may need
more)
green onions, finely
chopped

Use the same procedure as for the PLAIN THREE EGG OMELET. (See recipe.) Sauté the onions in the melted butter before adding the eggs.

CHEESE OMELET

3 eggs
3 tsp. cold water
2 drops Tabasco
salt and black pepper to
   taste

1 tbsp. butter
cheddar cheese, finely
   grated

Use the same procedure as for the PLAIN THREE EGG OMELET. (See recipe.) Add the finely grated cheese to the top of the omelet when the cooking is three-quarters complete. Fold the omelet over carefully onto the plate. The heat of the folded omelet will melt the cheese.

CHEESE SOUFFLÉ

2 tbsp. butter
3 tbsp. flour
1⅓ cups scalded milk
5 eggs, separated

½ tsp. salt
¼ tsp. black pepper
¾ cup grated cheddar
   cheese

Melt the butter in a pan over low to medium heat. Sprinkle the flour into the butter, carefully mix, and cook until it begins to bubble. Add the scalded milk and mix thoroughly. Remove from the heat and set aside.

Separate the eggs. Put four of the yolks into the butter and flour mixture. Add the salt and black pepper and mix thoroughly. Beat the whites until they are very stiff. Mix about ⅓ of the whites with the butter and flour mixture, along with the grated cheese. Combine the remaining ⅔ of the whites very loosely with the butter and flour. (Do not mix too thoroughly.)

Pour the mixture into a 1½-quart soufflé dish and put into a preheated 375-degree oven. Bake for 35 to 40 minutes and serve immediately.

MUSHROOM SOUFFLÉ

3 tbsp. butter
1 tbsp. chopped shallots
½ lb. finely chopped
    mushrooms
3 tbsp. flour

1 cup cold milk
1 tsp. salt
4 egg yolks
5 egg whites

Preheat the oven to 375°. Butter a 1½-quart soufflé dish.

Melt the butter in a skillet. Add the shallots and cook gently until the shallots are limp (about 5 minutes). Do not brown. Add the chopped mushrooms and simmer for 15 minutes. Add the flour and mix well; cook for 5 minutes over a very low heat. Add the milk and salt to the mushrooms and cook, stirring gently, until the mixture thickens. Remove from heat and allow to cool slightly. Add the egg yolks and blend well. Beat the egg whites until they are stiff but not dry and fold into the mushroom mixture. Pile the mixture lightly into the prepared soufflé dish and bake on the center rack of the oven for 25 to 30 minutes. Serves six.

GRAND MARNIER SOUFFLÉ

3 tbsp. butter
3 tbsp. flour
1 cup cold milk
grated rind of 1 orange
grated rind of 1 lemon

pinch of salt
⅓ cup Grand Marnier
8 egg whites
½ cup sugar
6 egg yolks

Preheat the oven to 375°. Butter and sugar a 1½-quart soufflé dish.

Melt the butter in a heavy, 2-quart saucepan; add the flour. Cook until the mixture is bubbling and golden. Remove from the stove and add the milk. Return to the heat and cook, stirring, until the sauce is thick and smooth. Add the grated lemon and orange rind and salt. Allow to cool slightly. Add the egg yolks and beat until smooth. Add the liqueur. Beat the egg whites until frothy; add the sugar gradually while beating the whites until stiff and glossy. Fold the whites carefully into the custard.

Pile the mixture into the prepared soufflé dish. Bake for 25 to 30 minutes. Serve at once to six or seven people.

*vegetables
and
grains*

"When the frost is on the pumpkin" makes for good poetry, but certainly plays havoc with the mirliton vines. So before Jack Frost spreads his mantle of white over the vines, it might be a good idea to get yourself a dozen or so of those "mellataws" (as we call them down South) and try different ways of cooking them. Mirlitons, vegetable pears, are a most versatile viand. They can be fried, boiled, baked, used in salads, pickled, steamed, smothered, stewed, and even baked into pies.

One well-known way to fix them is to first boil them for about 10 minutes. (They can't be real soft.) Then peel them, extract and discard the large seed in the center, and cut the fruit into bite-sized pieces. Beat up two eggs. Season the fruit with salt and pepper, dip the pieces into the eggs, then roll in cracker crumbs. If these pieces are then deep fried to a golden brown and sprinkled lightly with salt you have something which, as they say in the commercials is "Mmmmmm, good."

And how about a mirliton salad? Take ½ dozen, cut each one in half, then boil them in salted water until they are tender. Peel the pears and slice. Mix 5 tablespoons olive oil, 2 tablespoons vinegar, ½ teaspoon mustard, salt, and pepper. Pour this dressing over the slices. A delicious salad!

Or try mirliton pickles. Peel the mirlitons and get rid of the seeds. Now slice into long pieces and put in a jar. Heat in a glass or stainless steel pot enough water and vinegar (half and half) to cover the slices. Chop a couple of toes of garlic, and gather together a bay leaf, 5 or 6 whole allspice, salt, black pepper, and ¼ teaspoon cayenne pepper. Put all these seasonings in the vinegar and water and boil for about 10 minutes. Get the glass jar hot by setting it in hot water, then pour the vinegar and water combination into the jar with the sliced mirlitons. Cap tightly and wait no less than three weeks for the crunchiest pickles you ever tasted!

Of course, the classic way of fixing mirliton is stuffed. Take about 6 or 8 mirlitons and boil until they are tender. (You can check with a fork.) Meanwhile, put 2 tablespoons butter or margarine and 2 tablespoons oil into a frying pan, together with 1½ cups finely chopped onions, ¼ cup finely minced green onions, and ½ cup chopped green peppers. Let the vegetables sauté until very soft. Take the mirlitons out of the boiling water, cool, and cut in half lengthwise. Remove the large seed in the center and carefully scoop out the pulp. Leave the shell about a ¼-inch thick. Add the pulp to the sautéed onions and peppers and cook about 15 minutes over a medium fire. During the cooking, add 1 cup bread crumbs, 1 teaspoon sweet basil, a pinch of powdered thyme, a couple of shakes of Tabasco, and black pepper and garlic salt to taste.

Add one of the following: 1 cup chopped shrimp, 1 cup chopped, boiled ham, or 1½ cups of your favorite sausage (fried), and cook for another 10 minutes. Add a raw egg and stir until the egg is thoroughly blended into the mixture. Fill the shells with the mixture and sprinkle with bread crumbs. Dot with butter, put in the oven, and bake at 350° until bread crumbs are browned. Serves six to eight.

FRIED MIRLITON

mirlitons
2 eggs, beaten
cracker crumbs

salt and pepper to taste
cooking oil

MIRLITON SALAD

½ doz. mirlitons
5 tbsp. olive oil
2 tbsp. vinegar

½ tsp. mustard
salt and pepper to taste

MIRLITON PICKLES

mirlitons
vinegar and water (half and
    half, enough to cover the
    mirlitons)
a few toes garlic, chopped

1 bay leaf
5 or 6 whole allspice
salt
black pepper
¼ tsp. cayenne pepper

STUFFED MIRLITON

6 to 8 mirlitons
2 tbsp. butter or margarine
2 tbsp. oil
1½ cups finely chopped
   onions
¼ cup finely minced green
   onions
½ cup chopped green
   pepper
1 cup bread crumbs
1 tsp. sweet basil

a pinch of powdered thyme
couple of shakes of Tabasco
black pepper and garlic salt
   to taste
1 cup chopped shrimp
   (optional)
1 cup chopped, boiled ham
   (optional)
1½ cups fried sausage
   (optional)
1 egg

With appropriate modesty, I have to admit that Memere and Mamete were embodiments of complete Creole cooks, because in addition to knowing what to do with any ingredient that crossed their chopping boards, they also grew many of the seasonings and vegetables they used in their cooking.

Memere always set aside a little patch on "la terre bonne" where she grew her thyme, basil, mint, and tarragon. In the backyard she had a laurel tree, from which a branch was hung in the kitchen for her bay leaves. She also had a row or two of scallions, onions, and carrots, in addition to about ½ dozen carefully nurtured tomato plants.

Long before plant psychologists discovered it, Memere used to say that plants were like people—if you loved them, they would thrive. I'd swear that even the bugs cooperated with Memere and went to eat someone else's tomatoes! Or else they waited 50 years and are now eating mine!

Those gals used pure versatility in Creole cooking with the Creole tomatoes. They sliced them into salads, stewed them, broiled them, stuffed them, pureed them, and, of course, used them in soups, sauces, and gravies. Two of the dishes I remember being particularly delicious were STUFFED TOMATOES and TOMATOES AU GRATIN.

For the au gratin tomatoes, first scald and skin 6 large tomatoes, then cut into slices about ¼-inch thick. Place a layer of the slices in the bottom of a casserole dish and top with a layer of seasoned bread crumbs. (You can put the crumbs on rather thickly and then salt and pepper each layer.) Dot each layer with thin slices of butter. Alternate the layers of tomatoes and bread crumbs until you have used all the slices. Bake in a preheated 350-degree oven for 50 minutes. Simple, n'est ce pas?

For the stuffed tomatoes, you will need ½ dozen large specimens. Wipe them well with a damp towel and cut one slice close to the stem end of each. Scrape out the inside very carefully with a teaspoon. Put what you have scooped out in a dish and save.

Chop fairly finely an onion and a couple slices of boiled ham. Melt 2 tablespoons butter in a saucepan, add the onion and ham combination, and sauté slowly for about 5 minutes. Add the insides of the tomatoes, 1 cup seasoned bread crumbs, and ½ cup consommé or beef bouillon. Mix well, add salt and pepper to taste, and ½ teaspoon basil.

Cook over very low heat for 15 minutes and then allow to cool. Spoon the mixture into the tomato shells, sprinkle the tops with a few bread crumbs, and dot with butter. Preheat the oven to 350° and place the whole conglomerate therein for 15 to 20 minutes, or until the tops are slightly brown.

This is a real treat served hot with a beef or chicken dish. Serves six.

CREOLE TOMATOES AU GRATIN

6 large tomatoes	butter
seasoned bread crumbs	salt and pepper to taste

STUFFED CREOLE TOMATOES

½ doz. large tomatoes
1 onion, finely chopped
a few slices boiled ham,
  finely chopped
2 tbsp. butter
1 cup seasoned bread
  crumbs

½ cup beef consommé or
  beef bouillon
salt and pepper to taste
½ tsp. basil

I don't remember where I read it, so I can't credit the author with the statistic that the egg is the most universally used food worldwide. Second place went to the eggplant. This was a surprise to me at first, until I began to think of the wonderful ways the eggplant is used by people in every country. Consider dishes of the Far East built around the eggplant, also the great French and Italian dishes. I began to realize that no school of cooking is without its many ways of cooking eggplant.

And the Creoles were no exception. Memere would take them, young and tender, right off her little bushes (she always planted a patch in the spring) and make delectable hors d'oeuvres in a matter of minutes. To make these, just peel the eggplant, slice into pieces about ¼-inch thick, and then dip in beaten egg and in bread crumbs. Fry until brown, drain on paper, sprinkle with a little salt or Parmesan cheese, and that's it!

The Creoles had a dozen ways of stuffing the eggplant with vegetables, cheese, shrimp, crabmeat, beef, or pork, and then combinations of the aforementioned. Or, if we really wanted to dine elegantly on eggplant, nothing surpassed Memere's recipe for **EGGPLANT, OYSTER, AND MUSHROOM CASSEROLE**.

You begin with 2 medium eggplants. Preheat the oven to 350°. Before putting the eggplants in the oven, stick them a few times with a fork. This allows the vegetable to release the steam that builds up during the baking. Bake the eggplants for at least ½ hour, or until they are very tender. Test with a large fork.

Remove from the oven and allow to cool. While the eggplants cool, assemble the following ingredients:

3 doz. oysters and their water	**1 cup seasoned bread crumbs**
1½ sticks butter	**1 tsp. basil**
1 bunch shallots, chopped	**½ tsp. powdered thyme**
½ lb. fresh mushrooms, sliced	**salt and pepper to taste**
3 toes garlic, minced	**1 cup grated cheddar cheese**
2 shakes Tabasco	**½ cup evaporated milk**

Dump the oysters and their water into a saucepan and cook until the oyster edges begin to curl. Remove the oysters with a slotted spoon, and add ½ stick butter, the mushrooms, and the shallots. Let simmer for 10 minutes. Meanwhile, chop the oysters rather finely. Add ½ cup bread crumbs and the Tabasco and return the oysters to the pot. Mix well and set aside.

Melt ½ stick butter in a skillet, add the shallots, and sauté over a low heat for 5 minutes. Add the parsley, garlic, and ½ cup bread crumbs. When well mixed, remove from the heat and add the basil, thyme, and salt and pepper.

We are now ready to assemble the casserole. Peel the eggplants and slice them across in ¼-inch slices. Cover the bottom of a 12-inch by 12-inch casserole dish with half the slices. Sprinkle over this half the bread crumb and onion mixture and on top of this spoon half the oyster and mushroom mixture. Repeat this process with another layer of each. Sprinkle the cheddar cheese on top of the casserole, then drip the evaporated milk on top of the cheese. Spread over this some bread crumbs and top with ½ stick butter, sliced into 12 or 15 pats.

Place the casserole dish in a preheated 350-degree oven. Bake for 20 to 30 minutes, then be ready for eggplant at its best! Serves four to six.

STUFFED EGGPLANT I

3 large eggplants
½ lb. bacon
1 lb. pork sausage
3 stalks celery, very finely
  chopped
1 large green pepper, very
  finely chopped
5 green onions, very finely
  chopped

¾ cup bread crumbs
½ stick butter
½ tsp. powdered thyme
2 tbsp. Worcestershire
  sauce
½ cup grated Parmesan
  cheese
1 egg

Split the eggplants in half lengthwise and place in boiling water; boil until tender (20 to 30 minutes). They may also be baked in the oven for approximately 45 minutes if the skins are punctured several times to prevent exploding. After cooking, remove from water and allow to cool. Scoop out the center part of the eggplants, being careful to avoid tearing the skins. Chop or slice the cooked eggplant into small pieces and set aside.

Fry the bacon in a heavy iron pot until very crisp; remove and set aside. Fry the pork sausage in the bacon grease until well cooked and browned. Pour off all but 3 tablespoons of the grease. Add the chopped onions, peppers, and celery to the browned sausage and sauté well. Pour in the thyme and Worcestershire sauce while cooking. When the vegetables are tender, add the bread crumbs and butter. Mix well and cook over medium heat for 5 minutes. Add the eggplant and cook until the mixture is fairly dry. (I usually add more bread crumbs to make a drier mixture.) Stir in 1 raw egg, then turn off the heat. Add the Parmesan cheese and the bacon (crumbled) and stir well.

Stuff the mixture into the eggplant skins. Place pats of butter on top of each and sprinkle generously with bread crumbs. Place on a cookie sheet and broil until crisp on top. Serve hot.

STUFFED EGGPLANT II

3 medium eggplants
olive oil
1 cup green onions,
  chopped
3 cloves garlic, chopped
1 cup onions, chopped
2 tsp. thyme
2 bay leaves
¼ cup plus 2 tbsp. butter
white bread to equal 2 cups
  after it has been
  moistened with water and
  squeezed dry

1½ cups coarsely chopped
  cooked ham or shrimp
3 eggs, slightly beaten
3 tbsp. chopped parsley
1 tsp. salt
¼ tsp. pepper
¼ cup dry bread crumbs
2 tbsp. grated Parmesan
  cheese
½ tsp. paprika

Place whole eggplants in a 350-degree oven for about 40 minutes. Cut the eggplants lengthwise and scoop out meat, being sure to keep the shell in its original shape. Sauté the shells in olive oil for about 3 minutes on each side.

Melt ¼ cup butter in a large skillet. Sauté the green onions, onions, garlic, thyme, and bay leaves. Mix in the bread, then add the chopped eggplant and ham or shrimp. Gradually add the eggs, stirring constantly. Mix in the parsley, salt, and pepper. Remove bay leaves.

Pile the mixture into the eggplant shells. Sprinkle with bread crumbs, cheese, and paprika, then dot with remaining 2 tablespoons butter. Bake in a 350-degree oven for 20 minutes. Makes six servings.

FRIED EGGPLANT

1 eggplant
2 eggs
½ cup milk
¼ tsp. Tabasco

seasoned bread crumbs
salt and pepper to taste
oil for frying

Peel the whole eggplant with a vegetable peeler, and slice horizontally into pieces about ¾ of an inch thick. Salt and pepper each slice to taste. Dip the slices first into a mixture of the eggs, milk, and Tabasco, and then into the bread crumbs. Deep fry slowly on both sides. Serves four to six.

Memere used to say as we slid into the hot days of summer, "Eat more okra, it cools the blood and it's good for the stomach." So in June and July when we went to market we always bought a couple of pounds of okra. Memere was very particular about okra. Only fresh, tender okra would she tolerate. She maintained that the large, tough okra was fibrous, had lost its food value, and played havoc with the stomach.

She would often tell the story of how the okra got to America. The okra was a favorite vegetable in Africa. When the slave traders began to raid the African colonies for their stock, some of the blacks, knowing they would be sold into slavery and not knowing what prospects there were for food, smuggled some of the okra seeds in their thick, bushy hair. The story also related the Bantu word for okra—kingombo, or gombo. From this you can see not only how we got the okra, but also how gumbo got its name. So much for okra history whose authenticity I cannot vouch for. Now let's cook some!

Okra is delicious just boiled until tender, cooled, and served with vinegar, oil, and salt and pepper. If you like it braised, take 1 pound of small, fresh okra, wash it thoroughly, and slice off the stems; drain until dry. In a heavy skillet, heat ¼ cup of bacon drippings until fairly hot. Add the okra and sauté, stirring frequently, until it is brown on all sides. Add ¼ teaspoon black pepper, 1 teaspoon salt, and ½ cup finely chopped shallots. Lower the heat, and when the onions are brown, add ½ cup beef broth. Lower the heat to simmer, cover the pot, and cook about 5 minutes more, or until the okra is very tender.

But our favorite way to cook okra (except in gumbo) was in a RATATOUILLE, a delectable combination of baby okra, tomatoes, and onions.

In your skillet, melt 2 tablespoons butter and 1 tablespoon olive oil. Add 2 large onions (finely chopped) and sauté slowly until brown. Add 2½ cups sliced baby okra and cook for about 10 minutes, stirring frequently. Slice 2 ripe tomatoes and add to the skillet, along with a shake of Tabasco, ½ cup finely chopped shallots, ½ teaspoon basil, ¼ teaspoon black pepper, and ¾ teaspoon salt. Mix thoroughly and let cook over low heat about 15 minutes. Cover the pan, but occasionally stir.

Serve hot with a nice hunk of French bread. Serves four to six.

BRAISED OKRA

1 lb. small, fresh okra
¼ cup bacon drippings
¼ tsp. black pepper

1 tsp. salt
½ cup finely chopped
   shallots
½ cup beef broth

RATATOUILLE

2 tbsp. butter
1 tbsp. olive oil
2 large onions, finely
   chopped
2½ cups baby okra, sliced
¼ tsp. black pepper

2 ripe tomatoes, sliced
1 shake Tabasco
½ cup finely chopped
   shallots
½ tsp. basil
¾ tsp. salt

FRENCH FRIED OKRA

2 lbs. fresh, young okra
2 eggs, beaten
¼ tsp. Tabasco
1 tsp. garlic salt

1 tbsp. Lea & Perrins
white cornmeal
salt
cooking oil

Cut the ends off the okra and boil for about 8 minutes. Beat the eggs into a bowl, and add Tabasco, garlic salt, and Lea & Perrins. Dip the okra first into the egg mixture and then into the cornmeal. (Completely cover with the cornmeal.) Fry in oil until done, remove, and sprinkle with salt.

CREOLE OKRA

2 lbs. okra, diced
oil
2 onions, chopped
½ tsp. basil
3 tbsp. butter

3 shallots, finely chopped
1 1-lb. can tomatoes
cayenne pepper and garlic
salt to taste

Fry the okra in a small amount of oil. Add the onions; sauté until tender. Add the rest of the ingredients and cook for about 10 minutes. Serves six.

How wonderful it is that in later life, many little things trigger memories of happy days of our past, little things that sometimes seem to be totally unrelated to the image or experience they bring back to us. Mamete had three "maiden" aunts. Her old aunts, as she called them, were three sisters whose real names I never knew. They were called Nannan, Tahtay and Noonoose. (I spell the names phonetically.) They lived in a small house somewhere on St. Philip Street a few blocks on the lake side of Claiborne. Tahtay was my godmother and so I was a sort of special person to her. Whenever Mamete and I visited the aunts (twice a month), I usually left with a little package of goodies fixed especially for the godchild.

The house in which these three lived was very small, but had a carefully tended herb garden. Along the side of the house was an alley, about half of which was paved. In the half that wasn't paved (along the fence), thyme grew in abundance. As one walked along the alley to get to the side entrance, some of the thyme which had crept out of its bed and into the sidewalk was crushed underfoot. Since the alley was used many times through the day there was always the cloying, pleasant odor of the crushed thyme just outside of the house. Even today, many years hence, the smell of thyme evokes the image of that little cottage and those three old gals on St. Philip Street.

But there was another aspect of our visits which also stuck in my memory. Inside the house were four rooms—a kitchen, two bedrooms, and a parlor. The parlor was used only on very special occasions and rarely was I allowed to enter it. It was always closed off. Even though the front door of the house opened into the parlor, our entrance was always through the side. The blinds were always drawn and the windows closed. On the very few occasions when I was allowed into this room, it was only for a short time. What impressed me so much about this room was that in my child's mind I smelled God's presence! In one corner of the room stood a table on which a crucifix stood upright. The room also had numerous small holy pictures and various medals. In the center of the table burned a votive light. It was set in a ruby-colored holder, and since the room was always dark, strange red designs could be seen along the walls. There seemed to be some sort of scented oil burning in the lamp whose strange sweet odor filled the room. This, to me, was the smell of God! This same feeling is reenacted today whenever I happen to smell some of the scented votive candles. As I said, I was allowed a quick look into the parlor, and then hurried back to the kitchen where Nannan would be fixing something to eat.

One of the dishes Nannan fixed—one of my favorites—was her BELL PEPPER CASSEROLE.

BELL PEPPER CASSEROLE

4 tbsp. oil
2 lbs. ground beef
6 bell peppers, finely
  chopped
3 onions, chopped
¼ cup chopped green
  onions
3 toes garlic, minced
4 slices stale French bread
1 cup seasoned bread
  crumbs

2 eggs, slightly beaten
½ tsp. powdered thyme
1 pinch powdered cloves
1 pinch powdered allspice
2 tbsp. minced parsley
1 dash hot pepper sauce
salt and black pepper to
  taste

Put the oil in a Dutch oven and slowly cook the meat over medium heat until it is brown. Remove the meat and set aside. Add the peppers, onions, and green onions and sauté until soft. Return the meat to the pot and mix in with the peppers and onions. Add the garlic.

Soak the stale bread in water until soft; squeeze out the water. Add the bread to the pot and mix well. Stir in the seasoned bread crumbs and remove from the heat. Add the slightly beaten eggs and stir until well mixed. Add the thyme, cloves, allspice, parsley, pepper sauce, and salt and pepper. When everything is well blended, place the mixture in a two-quart casserole. Sprinkle the top lightly with bread crumbs and place in a 350-degree oven for about 20 minutes or until thoroughly heated.

This should serve about six.

STUFFED PEPPERS

½ cup rice
6 bell peppers
1 lb. ground meat
½ stick butter
2 onions, chopped
2 green onions, chopped
½ tsp. beef bouillon
(granules)
2 pinches basil

2 shakes Tabasco
½ tsp. garlic salt
1 16-oz. can of tomatoes
½ tsp. chili powder
½ cup grated cheddar
cheese
⅓ cup grated Parmesan
cheese
⅛ tsp. cayenne pepper

First, put the rice on to boil in your rice cooker. Next, cut off the tops of the bell peppers and clean out the insides. Boil the peppers in plain water for 8 to 10 minutes until soft. Brown the ground meat in butter. Drain all but about 2 tablespoons of the liquid; add the onions and green onions and sauté. Sprinkle in the beef bouillon, basil, Tabasco, garlic salt, and chili powder. Add the tomatoes, rice, cayenne pepper, and grated cheeses to the meat sauce and mix well.

Stuff the peppers with this mixture and place them in a pan. Add enough water to cover the bottom of the pan. Bake 25 to 30 minutes at 350°. Will serve eight to ten.

CREOLE STUFFED ARTICHOKES

4 medium-sized artichokes
½ stick butter
4 shallots, finely chopped
¼ cup finely chopped
onions
1 cup cooked and deveined
shrimp

1½ cups seasoned bread
crumbs
salt
4 tbsp. lemon juice
1 egg, beaten
2 shakes Tabasco
olive oil

With a knife or scissors, cut off about the top third of the artichokes. Pull off some of the large, tough outer leaves around the bottom. Open the center and clean out all the fuzzy leaves (called the choke) all the way down to the heart. You can scrape the heart in the center, very gently, with a spoon. Cut off the stem flush with the base and stand the vegetables on their bases in a saucepan so they will fit snugly. Add a tablespoon of salt, 2 tablespoons lemon juice, and boiling water to cover. Cover and simmer for ½ hour. Remove the artichokes from the water, turn upside down, and let drain.

Put the butter and 2 tablespoons olive oil in a skillet; sauté the shallots and onions for about 5 minutes. Remove from heat and add the bread crumbs. Chop the shrimp into small pieces, and add to the skillet along with 1 teaspoon salt, the rest of the lemon juice, Tabasco, and the beaten egg. Mix well and then spoon the mixture into the artichokes.

Place the artichokes into a small pan; pour boiling water in the pan to a depth of about 1 inch. Brush the artichokes liberally with olive oil, cover with aluminum foil, and bake 30 minutes in a preheated 350-degree oven. Serves four to six.

STUFFED CUCUMBERS

½ lb. sliced bacon
4 medium cucumbers, peeled
1 onion, finely chopped
2 medium tomatoes, diced
4 shallots, finely chopped

¾ cup seasoned bread crumbs
1½ tsp. salt
¼ tsp. black pepper
2 shakes Tabasco
½ cup butter

Fry the bacon until it is crisp. Slice each cucumber lengthwise in half and scoop out the inside with a spoon, reserving about half the pulp. Finely chop the cucumber pulp; mix the pulp with ½ the chopped onion, ½ the tomatoes, the shallots, bread crumbs, salt, pepper, Tabasco, and 4 slices of the bacon, crumbled. Mix well and then fill the cucumber shells with the mixture.

Place in a shallow baking dish the rest of the bacon, crumbled, the rest of the onions, and the tomatoes. Put the stuffed cucumbers on top, then add ¼ cup of water to the bottom of the dish. Put a dot of butter on the top of each cucumber. Bake in a 350-degree oven 45 minutes to 1 hour, until the cucumbers are tender. Will serve six to eight.

Monday was always washday for Memere and Mamete. The week's washing was usually put to soak the night before in a large, galvanized tub. About ½ bar of Octagon soap was shaved in thin pieces into the water, and stirred into the wash. Come Monday morning washday would begin. The procedure usually involved three large tubs—the tub in which the clothes had been soaking and in which they would be scrubbed on a washboard, another tub filled with water in which the clothes were rinsed, and the third tub filled with water to which a few spoonfuls of bluing had been added. A small tub of thick, sticky starch would be cooking on the stove. After being washed, some of the clothes were dipped into the starch and then hung out to dry. From this you can see that washday was a laborious, complicated process, not at all like throwing clothes into a washer and flipping a switch.

Also, many times the white clothes had to be boiled! This happened once or twice a month, when they began to assume a dingy, gray hue. They were boiled in a kettle over a charcoal fire with a little soap added to the water, then rinsed and dipped in the bluing water before being hung out to dry. Being involved in such an all day operation left very little time for cooking. Thus, the custom developed of cooking red beans and rice on Mondays, a custom which holds even today.

Let me assure you that red beans and rice is not inferior, in any way, to even the finest of the Creole haute cuisine. Cooked in the manner I will describe in a moment, it is fare for even the most exacting gourmet. It also demonstrates the Creole cook's ability to serve an elegant meal at a very small expense. I remember Papete talking about going to the store for a nickel of beans, a "quartee" of rice, and a hambone. A "quartee," as he explained it, was an actual coin in use in the middle eighteen-hundreds which represented half a nickel. A pot of beans for four to six people, along with rice (a complete meal), would cost about twenty cents. And while the housewife did her washing, the beans simmered on the stove.

A pot of beans today will certainly cost more, but cooked the following way it is a meal which, as Memere would say, "will stick to your ribs." For creamy, **CREOLE RED BEANS** you will need:

1 thick slice raw ham	**2 bay leaves**
1 slice pickled pork	**½ tsp. powdered thyme**
1 lb. red kidney beans	**⅛ tsp. powdered allspice**
2 onions, chopped	**⅛ tsp. powdered cloves**
1 bell pepper, chopped	**½ tsp. chili powder**
3 ribs celery, chopped	**⅛ tsp. cayenne pepper**
4 cloves garlic, minced	**¼ tsp. black pepper**
1 tsp. sugar	**salt to taste**
2 tsp. vinegar	

Put the raw ham and pickled pork in a heavy pot and cover with 2½ quarts of cold water. Set the pot on a low heat; while it is heating, clean the beans. Take a handful at a time and pick out the gravel, dirt, and other particles. Rinse the beans and add to the pot. Chop the onions, bell pepper, celery, and garlic and add to the pot. Add all the seasonings except the salt. (Add the salt only after the beans have cooked for at least 3 hours.) Never let the mixture boil, but rather allow it to simmer gently. Stir the pot 3 to 4 times an hour.

As the beans begin to soften, mash some of them against the side of the pot. The result will be a thick, creamy sauce. (You will note we did not add sausage to the beans. At the risk of heresy, let me advise you not to cook your sausage in the beans. Fry it and serve along with the beans. The taste is so much better.) When the beans have cooked to a creamy tenderness they are ready to serve over fluffy, white rice.

Before you serve, first slice 2 white onions very thin, add 3 tablespoons olive oil, 1 tablespoon vinegar, and some salt and black pepper. When you serve the beans and rice, add a spoon or two of the onion salad right on top. Serves six to eight.

RED BEANS AND RICE

If you insist on cooking sausage with your red beans, try this recipe.

1 lb. dried red beans
2 qts. water
1 meaty ham bone or
thickly sliced raw ham,
cubed
1 lb. hot sausage
2 cups chopped onions
1 bunch green onions,
chopped

1 bell pepper, chopped
2 stalks celery, chopped
4 bay leaves
pinch of thyme
Tabasco to taste
salt and pepper to taste

Rinse the red beans and pick out any bad ones. Cover with the water and set on a medium heat. Add the ham bone and sausage. As this cooks, add the onions, bell pepper, celery, shallots, and seasonings. Lower the heat to a simmer after the beans come to a boil; simmer for several hours.

Use a wooden spoon to mash a quantity of beans on the side of the pot. This will produce a creamy smoothness characteristic of Creole red beans. After about 4 hours, they will be ready to serve over rice.

CHOU GLORIEUX

1 large or 2 small heads of
cabbage
2 onions, finely chopped
1 bell pepper, chopped
½ cup chopped green
onions
¾ cup bread crumbs
4 ribs celery, chopped
½ pt. cream

½ stick butter or margarine
1 tbsp. cooking oil
4 cloves garlic, minced
3 slices toasted bread
½ lb. grated cheddar cheese
2 tbsp. minced parsley
salt and black pepper to
taste
milk

Cut the cabbage into fourths and cut out the tough center; parboil until tender. When tender, drain and slice into small pieces. Melt the butter in a saucepan or skillet, add the oil, and sauté the onions, green onions, celery, and bell pepper until they are limp. Add the cabbage, cover, and over a very low heat cook for about 10 minutes, stirring once or twice. Uncover and add all but about ¼ cup of the grated cheese. Stir well and allow to cook a few more minutes.

In the meantime, soak the toasted bread in milk until soft, then squeeze out the milk, and add to the cabbage. Add the cream, half of the bread crumbs, garlic, and parsley; remove from the heat and mix well. Add salt and pepper.

Place the mixture in a casserole dish. Mix the remaining bread crumbs and the cheese and sprinkle over the cabbage. Bake in a preheated 350-degree oven, uncovered, for about 30 minutes. This will serve six to eight.

STEAMED CABBAGE

1 large cabbage, shredded
2 onions, chopped
2 beef bouillon cubes
garlic salt and pepper to
    taste

4 shallots, chopped
½ tsp. basil
2 tbsp. Worcestershire
    sauce

Sauté the onions slowly in a dry pot. (No oil is used in this dish.) When done, add 1 cup water with the 2 beef bouillon cubes melted in it. Add the cabbage. Season with the herbs.

Steam about 5 minutes, stir, and steam 4 or 5 minutes more. Add garlic salt, pepper, and Worcestershire sauce. Stir well and serve to four to six people.

BUTTERED OKRA

1 cup water
1 lb. fresh okra
½ tsp. salt

½ lemon
2 tbsp. butter
¼ tsp. pepper

Boil okra in water with salt and lemon. (Do not squeeze the lemon.) Cook until okra is tender (almost 20 minutes). Drain off any water left, place over low flame, and add butter. When butter is melted, add pepper, remove lemon and serve. Serves four to six.

FETTUCINE ALFREDO

1 lb. fettucine noodles
1 cup unsalted butter
1 cup freshly grated
  Parmesan cheese

½ cup heavy cream
freshly ground black pepper

Cook the fettucine in boiling, salted water until "al dente" (literally, "with a little tooth"—a slight hardness in the center), about 8 to 10 minutes, then drain. Heat the butter in a saucepan until barely melted. Add the noodles, remove from the heat, and toss. Add the Parmesan and toss again over a low heat. When well mixed, add the cream and continue tossing until the mixture is very hot. Sprinkle with black pepper and serve at once. Serves four to six.

BALLED AND BUTTERED POTATOES

several potatoes, peeled
salt and black pepper to
  taste

1 stick butter
1 tbsp. cooking oil

Scoop the peeled potatoes into balls with a melon baller, letting them fall into cold water to keep them from turning black. Drain in colander and dry well. Place in a mixing bowl and add salt and black pepper to taste. Melt the butter, add the cooking oil, and pour over the potatoes. Mix until all are well coated. Spread on a cookie sheet and broil until golden brown, turning occasionally.

BRABANT POTATOES

potatoes
cooking oil

salt and black pepper to
  taste

Peel the potatoes and cut into uniform cubes (approximately ¾-inch cubes) so that they will all cook in the same amount of time. Place potato cubes into salted boiling water; boil until they are tender but still firm enough to hold together. Remove and drain well. Dump the cubes into very hot cooking oil and fry until they are golden brown. (Do not add too many at one time to the cooking oil.) Remove when brown, place on absorbent paper towels, and add salt and black pepper to taste. Serve while hot.

It is very disconcerting to me (and probably you, too) to sit down to a meal and discover a cold, gooey blob of something that's called mashed potatoes. Such a situation will usually deter one from an appreciation, no matter how well fixed, of the balance of the meal. This doesn't have to be. It is not at all difficult to serve fluffy, creamy, hot mashed potatoes with just a few simple instructions.

CREOLE MASHED POTATOES are so delicious with a sauce piquante, a courtbouillon, or even grillades, and yet I really believe that their loss in popularity can be attributed to the difficulty most cooks have in serving them just right. Memere had a wonderful recipe that would certainly eliminate this problem. If you try it, I know you will like it. This will serve four.

Peel 5 large or 6 or 7 medium-sized potatoes, then cut into smaller pieces and put into a pot with a couple of quarts of water. Add a teaspoon of salt and a large onion, finely chopped. Let this come to a boil, then simmer until the potatoes are tender; drain. Don't, under any circumstances, throw away the water in which the potatoes were boiled. This will make a wonderful stock for soup or gumbo or even the liquid for a jambalaya.

Now put the potatoes in a large bowl along with ½ stick butter and begin to mash. My preference in "mashers" is the old-fashioned wooden kind. When the potatoes are almost mashed, add a raw egg and continue to mash to the consistency you prefer. Add salt and black pepper to taste and set aside until ready to serve.

When you are ready to eat the potatoes, boil about 2 cups of milk. When the milk froths up, add carefully to the potatoes, stirring the while until they are as creamy as you want them. You can serve hot, creamed mashed potatoes at any time. If you make too much, put the leftovers in the refrigerator and the next day they'll be perfect for codfish balls or a base for some vichysoisse.

So much for Memere's mashed potatoes. Lest you begin to believe that I live only in the culinary past, let me pass on Missy's recipe for STUFFED POTATOES. Who's Missy? Why, she's my daughter, Yvette, and one of the best little cooks that ever graced a Creole kitchen. I'm sure that Memere looks down from that great Creole kitchen in the sky and smiles with satisfaction as she watches her great-granddaughter at work.

To prepare Missy's stuffed potatoes, first wash and dry (very well) five medium to large baking potatoes. Then rub them with a light coating of cooking oil and put them in a preheated 375-degree oven. Bake until the potatoes are cooked inside. Check with a fork; if the fork goes in easily, the potatoes are done. (This should take an hour or longer.)

In the meantime, fry ¼ pound of bacon until it is crisp and set aside.

In the bacon grease, sauté 1 cup finely chopped onion and ½ cup finely chopped shallots. Cook over a very low fire until the vegetables are well done. In a bowl, meanwhile, let two 3-ounce packages Philadelphia cream cheese get to room temperature. Dump the sautéed vegetables on top.

When the potatoes are done, remove them from the oven, split them in half lengthwise, and begin to scoop out the interior. Leave about ⅛ inch of potato inside. Set the shells aside and mix the potato insides with ½ stick butter and the cream cheese and vegetables. When thoroughly mixed add salt and pepper to taste. Add 1 cup hot milk, mix well, then crumble the bacon and add to the mixture.

Take a tablespoon and begin to fill in the shells. When this is finished, top off each potato with about 1 tablespoon of grated cheddar cheese and a sprinkling of paprika. Run in the oven for a couple of minutes to melt the cheese on top and then you're ready to enjoy Missy's stuffed potatoes. Serves eight to ten.

CREOLE MASHED POTATOES

5 large or 6 or 7 medium-
   sized potatoes
a few qts. water
salt
1 raw egg

1 large onion, finely
   chopped
½ stick butter
black pepper to taste
2 cups milk

MISSY'S STUFFED POTATOES

5 medium to large baking
   potatoes
cooking oil
¼ lb. bacon
1 cup finely chopped onion
1 cup hot milk
1 tbsp. grated cheddar
   cheese

½ cup finely chopped
   shallots
2 3-oz. pkgs. Philadelphia
   cream cheese
salt and pepper to taste
sprinkle of paprika
½ stick butter

I remember an interesting story Mamete related to me about how the potato was introduced to the French cooks. It seems that the French king, Francis, knew about the potato, had eaten and enjoyed it, and wanted to introduce it to the populace. But even in that day, human perversity was as universal as it is today, and the French would not accept the vegetable.

Being the wise king that he was, Francis hit upon a plan that worked! The first thing he did was publicize the fact that the potato, being such a magnificent vegetable, was fit only for the royal taste and should not be eaten by commoners. He then proceeded to grow the tubers on the palace grounds and issued an edict forbidding anyone to grow potatoes outside the palace walls. I think you can guess the rest. And so the French became potato eaters. They transferred this preference to the Creoles, and we have eaten those delectable vegetables ever since.

Memere had a way of using leftover mashed potatoes that was really a joy to behold and taste. She would use 2 cups of cold mashed potatoes and mix them well in a frying pan with 3 tablespoons butter. When this was well mixed, she would stir in 2 well-beaten egg yolks and 3 tablespoons of cream. She stirred this for awhile until well mixed, then removed from the heat and added the stiffly beaten whites of the eggs. Next she buttered a baking dish and filled it with the mixture. This was baked in a 375-degree oven until brown on top. This is an old Creole recipe and one we truly enjoyed.

Sometimes, for dessert, Mamete would give us a special treat and fix her apples stuffed with sweet potatoes. Boy, how we loved it! She used 3 large, red apples. First, she cut them in half crosswise, and removed the core and seeds. Then she sprinkled each cavity with 1 teaspoon brown sugar.

The apples were put in a shallow pan containing about ¼ inch water and baked in a 400-degree oven for 15 minutes.

The apple halves were then scooped out, leaving a shell about ¼ inch thick. (Hold on to the pulp, you'll be needing it.) To 3 cups of cooked, mashed sweet potatoes, add the apple pulp, 3 tablespoons butter, and 3 tablespoons cream and beat until fluffy. A little more sugar can also be added if you prefer.

Pile the potato mixture into the apple shells, place in the shallow pan, sprinkle with a little brown sugar, then dot with butter. Heat under the broiler or in a 400-degree oven until lightly brown. Our only problem here was how to eat the hot dessert before it had cooled enough. Don't you make that mistake. The potato and apple combination really holds its heat for a long time so be careful.

Serves six.

LEFTOVER MASHED POTATO CASSEROLE

2 cups cold mashed
  potatoes
3 tbsp. butter

2 eggs (separate yolks and
  whites)
3 tbsp. cream

APPLES STUFFED WITH SWEET POTATOES

3 large, red apples
1 tsp. brown sugar
3 cups cooked, mashed
  sweet potatoes

3 tbsp. butter
3 tbsp. cream

SWEET POTATO CAKES

2 cups cooked mashed
  sweet potatoes
1 egg, slightly beaten

½ cup chopped peanuts
flour
bacon drippings for frying

Mix together well the egg and potatoes; add the peanuts. Form into small, flat cakes and dredge with flour. Heat the bacon drippings in a heavy frying pan and fry the cakes, turning once, until lightly browned.

Serves six to eight.

As I've said, many of the Creole's greatest delights were served over rice. This is where the Creoles shone, because nowhere in the world was the preparation of rice taken so seriously and done so magnificently as in the Creole household. The objective in cooking rice was to have it turn out light and fluffy, grain for grain, not sticky.

One of the ways this was done was first of all by "using the best quality of rice," that is, the long grain rice. This rice was rinsed at least five or six times until the water became clear. It wasn't a question of the rice being dirty, but rather of washing all the starch off of it. The rice was washed and picked for any little impurities. Then it was put into a regular rice pot. The Creoles always designated one certain pot for cooking rice. This was usually a thick bottomed, thick sided pot, sometimes a cast iron pot, and was used *only* for cooking rice.

The rice was washed and put into the pot, and a carefully measured amount of water was added. This is the way it was done. The Creole cooks spread the rice evenly on the bottom of the pot and added water until the water approached the depth up to the first joint of the index finger. In other words, regardless of how much raw rice was used in the pot, water was added until it was deep enough to come up to the first joint after touching the top of the rice with the forefinger. Then a pad of asbestos was put over the burner and the pot of rice placed on top. (All Creole kitchens had these pads used for cooking rice.) As soon as the water began to boil, the heat was turned as low as possible. The pot was covered and the rice allowed to cook for at least 20 minutes. After 20 minutes, the rice was fluffed with a fork and about a tablespoon or so of lard was stirred into the pot. The pot was covered again and allowed to cook for another 20 minutes. After the second 20 minutes, the rice was uncovered and allowed to cool before being served.

The extra 20 minutes and the lard produced a brown crust around the bottom and sides of the pot. When the rice was served, it was dug out of the center. Of course, the crust was also served. As children, we always fought for the crust, because it was like getting a special treat such as a piece of cake.

The Creoles cooked rice other ways also. For a different way, start with a very large amount of water in proportion to the rice. For example, if you were cooking 2 cups of rice, put it into about 3 quarts of water. Bring the water to a rolling boil and then slowly add the rice so you do not disrupt the boiling of the water. Let the water continue to boil as rapidly as possible. Cook the rice about 14 to 15 minutes. Check periodically so that it is not cooked too long.

This rice was cooked "al dente" as the Italians say, or "little tooth" when drained. The rice was drained in a colander and then rinsed in cold water. The colander was immediately put on top of a pot in which water was boiling. The rice was allowed to steam for 5 to 10 minutes. The steam dried the rice and made it very fluffy.

Another simple way to cook rice was to take just about twice as much water as rice, and put it into the saucepan. Let it boil 2 to 4 minutes, and then turn the fire down as low as possible. Cover the rice and cook for about 15 minutes. Add a few pinches of salt and a tablespoon or so of butter or margarine if desired. This again will produce nice, fluffy rice.

DIRTY RICE

1 lb. chicken gizzards
1 lb. chicken livers
6 cups water or chicken
  stock
1 tsp. salt
1 tbsp. Worcestershire
  sauce
1 tsp. red pepper
3 tbsp. bacon drippings,
  oil, or margarine

1 bunch shallots, chopped
1 cup chopped celery
2 red peppers, finely
  chopped
1 lb. lean ground meat
2 lbs. hot bulk sausage
2 cups uncooked rice

Boil the gizzards and livers in water or stock to which the Worcestershire sauce, salt, and pepper has been added. Boil about 30 minutes, remove gizzards and livers (retaining the liquid), grind, and set aside. In a large Dutch oven, sauté the shallots, celery, and peppers in the bacon drippings until nicely browned. Brown the ground meat and the sausage in a separate pot; pour off the excess grease. Put the vegetables, gizzards, livers, meat, and sausage in the Dutch oven. Sauté slowly about 5 minutes. Add 4 cups of the reserved liquid and simmer slowly for about an hour. If it thickens too much, add a little more liquid.

Cook the rice in your rice cooker and mix with the meat mixture. Bake in a covered dish at 325° for 30 minutes. Serves fifteen to twenty.

GREEN RICE

3 cups cooked rice (may
   use leftover)
1½ cups grated cheddar
   cheese
½ cup finely chopped green
   onions
salt and pepper to taste

6 tbsp. melted butter
3 egg yolks, beaten
3 egg whites, stiffly beaten
3 tbsp. chopped onion
½ cup minced parsley

Mix all the above ingredients except the egg whites until thoroughly combined. Fold in the beaten egg whites. Grease a 1½-quart baking dish with butter and add the mixture. Preheat your oven to 350° and bake for 25 minutes. Will serve six.

BAKED CHEESE RICE

3 cups cooked rice
2 cups grated cheddar
   cheese
1 cup finely minced green
   pepper
½ cup finely minced
   shallots

2 eggs, beaten
1¼ cups milk
1 tsp. salt
¼ tsp. cayenne pepper
½ cup seasoned bread
   crumbs
1 tbsp. melted butter

Mix the green pepper and the shallots. Arrange alternate layers of cooked rice, cheese, and green peppers and shallots in a buttered baking dish. Mix together the eggs, milk, salt, and pepper and pour over the rice and cheese mixture. Mix the bread crumbs and butter and sprinkle over the top. Bake in a preheated 350-degree oven about 45 minutes or until set. Will serve four to six.

RIZ AU LAIT

This was a dish the Creoles prepared for breakfast with rice leftover from the previous day's meal.

1 cup cooked rice
2 cups simmering milk
¾ cup sugar

½ tsp. pure vanilla extract
nutmeg

Add the rice to the simmering milk and cook for 2 minutes. Add the sugar, stir well, and cook for another minute. Remove from the heat and add the vanilla extract. Mix thoroughly and place in a dish to cool. Sprinkle the top with nutmeg and serve at about room temperature. Will serve three to four people.

HUSH PUPPIES

cooking oil
2 cups flour
1½ cups cornmeal
½ tsp. salt
2 tsp. baking powder

1 tsp. sugar
2 eggs, well beaten
¾ cup milk
1 small onion, finely grated

Almost fill a deep frying pan with oil and place over moderate heat while preparing the batter. Heat should reach about 375° on a thermometer by the time you're ready to fry your hush puppies.

Combine flour, cornmeal, salt, baking powder, and sugar in a mixing bowl. Beat together the eggs, milk, and onions, then add to the dry mixture. Beat to a smooth batter. Drop by teaspoonfuls into the hot fat and fry until lightly browned. Remove and drain on paper towel.

CORNMEAL BATTER CAKES

1 cup cornmeal
½ tsp. salt
1 tsp. baking powder

1 egg, well beaten
1¼ cups buttermilk
oil or shortening

Sift the cornmeal, baking powder, and salt into a bowl. Mix in the egg and the buttermilk and stir until smooth. Heat a cast iron frying pan or griddle to better than moderate heat and grease the bottom with shortening or oil. Pour the batter onto the pan or griddle in small amounts (about 1 tablespoon of batter for each cake). Cook until the top begins to bubble, then turn and brown the other side. When the cakes are brown on both sides, remove and spread each cake with soft butter and a little molasses.

This amount of batter will make about 20 small cakes.

WHEAT GERM BREAD

1¼ cups scalded milk
1½ tsp. honey
1 tsp. salt
2 tsp. melted butter
1 pkg. yeast

¼ cup warm water
½ tsp. sugar
3½ cups unbleached white
    flour with wheat germ

Mix together in a bowl the milk, honey, salt, and melted butter. Stir until well mixed. Allow to cool. In a cup, dissolve the sugar in the warm water and then add the yeast. "Proof" the yeast by watching for a few minutes for the mixture to bubble. Add it to the milk mixture. Add a small amount of the flour at a time, beating well after each addition. When all the flour is mixed in, turn the dough on a lightly floured board. Knead the dough until smooth and elastic. Place the dough in a well-greased bowl; turn the dough to grease the top and cover with a damp towel.

Let the dough rise in a warm place until it doubles in size. Punch down. Let rise again until it doubles in size. Punch down again and then let rest for 10 minutes. Shape dough into loaf. Place in a 9-inch x

5-inch x 3-inch greased loaf pan. Brush the top of the loaf with short-ening, butter, or cooking oil. Cover, and let rise until almost double in size. Bake in a moderate oven (375°) until done, about 40 minutes. Yields 1 large loaf.

NOTE: I mentioned "white flour with wheat germ." There is a flour sold that meets that description. If you can't find it, use stone ground whole wheat flour.

CHEESE PUFFS

4 eggs
2 cups rich milk
butter
8 slices stale bread

sharp cheese (cheddar)
salt, pepper, and paprika to taste

Beat the eggs; add the milk and mix well. Butter the bread thickly and cut into pieces. Slice the cheese and place the pieces on the bread; season with the salt, pepper, and paprika.

Place the bread pieces in a casserole dish and pour the egg mixture slowly into the dish. You can top with more butter if you desire. Bake in a 400-degree oven for about 30 minutes or until puffed and firm in the center. Serve hot.

CORN DOGS

½ lb. spicy sausage meat
1 onion, finely chopped
1 tsp. chili powder
2 tbsp. consommé or beef
    stock
vegetable oil
1 cup cornmeal

½ cup flour
3 tbsp. baking powder
¼ tsp. salt
2 eggs
¾ cup milk
3 tbsp. melted and cooled
    butter

Cook the sausage meat and onion in a frying pan; sauté, stirring, until meat is brown. Add the chili powder and beef stock and cook over a medium heat until the liquid has been absorbed. Set aside.

Preheat the oven to 375°. Grease two cast iron cornstick pans generously with the vegetable oil and place them in the oven. Combine cornmeal, flour, baking powder, and salt in a mixing bowl. Beat the eggs, add to the milk, and blend in with the dry mixture. Add the melted butter and stir until blended.

Fill the hot cornstick pans about one-fourth full with the batter. Spoon some of the sausage mixture in the center and then cover with batter. Place in the 375-degree oven and bake 20 to 25 minutes or until lightly browned.

COUSH COUSH

2 cups yellow cornmeal
½ tsp. salt
1½ cups water

2 tsp. baking powder
3 eggs
1 tsp. oil

Heat the water to the boiling point in a saucepan. Add the salt and stir in the cornmeal. When well mixed, set aside to cool. When cool, add the baking powder. Beat the eggs well and add to the mixture. Put the oil or shortening in a skillet and when hot, pour in the cornmeal mixture. Cook over medium heat for about 5 minutes. Can be served as is or with molasses. Will serve six to eight.

desserts

Would you believe we had *two* sources of water? We had the regular city water and also a cistern! The cistern, a large wooden tank, about 6 feet in diameter and 6 feet in height, was in the back yard. It was connected to the roof gutters by a pipe, so that it could catch the rain water falling off of the roof.

Memere didn't like the taste of the tap water, and never used it in her cooking, to drip coffee, or to drink. She always used the cistern water to wash clothes, because the soap lathered so much better than with the tap water. She used regular water to rinse the clothes. At night, the pitchers on the washstand were always filled with cistern water. It was supposed to be better for your complexion.

Of course, these two sources of water only handled ordinary temperatures. Every bit of hot water we used had to be heated on the stove. Memere boiled it in her large copper kettle, one of her prize possessions. It had a long spout, and could accommodate about 3 gallons of water. Each time we took a bath, water had to be heated on the stove and then poured into the bathtub. Ah, what a blessing—today's water heater!

The water level in the cistern depended on the amount of rain that fell. Therefore, many times during a dry spell the water got very low. As the water got low, we began to get a little sludge out of the faucets. Sometimes we also got a few mosquito larvae ("wiggletails") in our water. Then it was time to clean the cistern. This was a pretty big job, and required the combined efforts of Pepere, Papete, and little Leon.

First of all, the water had to be drained. The drain was opened the day before the cleaning, and by morning of the next day, the tank was empty. Then, the conical metal top was removed. Either my father or my grandfather would get inside and scrub the tank. Finally, the tank was rinsed, the top put back on, and it was ready for the rain to "fill 'er up."

After we finished the chore, Memere would always have a baked treat ready to eat. When pumpkins were available, she made her PUMPKIN PECAN PIE.

PUMPKIN PECAN PIE

3 eggs
1 cup mashed, cooked
  pumpkin (If fresh
  pumpkin is not available,
  use the canned variety.)
1 cup sugar
½ cup corn syrup (dark is
  preferred)

1 tsp. vanilla
½ tsp. cinnamon
¼ tsp. salt
1 9-in. unbaked pastry shell
  (or try making the pastry
  yourself)
1 cup chopped pecans
whipped cream (optional)

First, beat the eggs slightly in a mixing bowl, then add the pumpkin, sugar, corn syrup, vanilla, cinnamon, and salt. Mix very well and then pour the mixture into the pie shell. Sprinkle the pecans over the top.

Bake for about 40 minutes in a preheated 350-degree oven. Test by inserting a knife halfway between the center and the edge. If the knife comes out clean, the pie is done. When the pie is done, chill.

This pie is "très simple" to prepare, and is most delicious when topped with a little whipped cream for a Bon Appetit!

The entire neighborhood knew when it was coffee roasting time in our house. That wonderful smell from the roasting beans seemed reluctant to do anything but hang around and slowly spread itself from house to house. Of course, the neighbors didn't mind because they also roasted their coffee on about a weekly basis.

Memere would always buy the raw beans at the store on about a monthly basis, and we'd roast just enough to last a week. She put about 5 cups of the beans in a black iron skillet in which a very small quantity of lard had been lightly rubbed. The skillet was put in the oven, and after a time, the delicious aroma of the roasting beans greeted our nostrils.

The beans were stirred a few times and soon were roasted to a chocolate brown color. They were then quickly cooled and put in an airtight jar. That would be our coffee for the week. Memere vowed that roasted beans were stale if kept any longer than a week.

Early each morning about ¾ of a cup of the roasted beans would be removed from the jar and put in the grinder. How I enjoyed turning the handle on the grinder and then removing the ground coffee to a bowl! There it was blended with a couple of tablespoons of roasted, ground chicory. Then, it would be poured into the little cloth bag sitting on top of the French drip coffee pot. We were now ready to drip the coffee.

First, a pot of water was brought to the boiling point. (In our house, this was cistern water. Memere claimed city water would ruin the taste of the coffee.) Two tablespoons (no more) of the boiling water were poured over the coffee, and then 4 or 5 minutes would elapse before the grounds ceased puffing and bubbling. (Pouring too much water at the beginning would have resulted in a weaker flavor.) Once the grounds had settled, a little of the boiling water was poured slowly at intervals until enough coffee had been brewed. A delightful aroma, meanwhile, had invaded half the house. Then came the hot, black demitasse of coffee with 2 or 3 teaspoons of sugar. What a marvelous eye opener! For a real morning treat, Memere would make some of her **CREAM CHEESE COFFEE CAKE**.

She mixed a cup of Creole cream cheese with 2 tablespoons of cream until the lumps were gone. Then she added 1 teaspoon baking soda and poured all this into a bowl. In another bowl, she creamed together ½ cup softened butter and 1 cup granulated sugar. To the sugar and butter she added 2 well-beaten eggs and 1 teaspoon of vanilla and mixed this well. Next, sifted together were 1¾ cups cake flour and 2 teaspoons baking powder. Added alternately to the sugar and butter mixture, a little at a time, were the flour mixture and the cream cheese mixture. When all this was mixed, the topping was prepared.

The topping was made by mixing ¼ cup brown sugar, 1 teaspoon cinnamon and ¼ cup chopped pecans.

Half of the batter was spread into an 8-inch square pan with half the topping spread on the batter. The rest of the batter then was added and atop this went the remainder of the topping mixture.

The cake was baked about 50 minutes in a preheated 350-degree oven. After about 40 minutes, a clean knife was inserted into the cake. If the knife came out clean, the cake was done. The cake was served warm with a cup of Café au Lait—no better way to start the day.

1 cup Creole cream cheese	**2 well-beaten eggs**
2 tbsp. cream	**1 tsp. vanilla**
1 tsp. baking soda	**1¾ cups cake flour**
½ cup softened butter	**2 tsp. baking powder**
1 cup granulated sugar	

TOPPING

¼ cup brown sugar	**¼ cup chopped pecans**
1 tsp. cinnamon	

During the hot summer months, Memere always used the oil stove for cooking. This was a stove that used kerosene as fuel. We bought the kerosene by the gallon and called it "coal oil." The average cost a week for cooking ran between 15 and 25 cents.

When the weather got cooler, we would "fire up" the wood stove. Then the kitchen became a treasure trove of baked goodies. The oven was always "on," or hot, whether it was used or not. It followed then that with very little trouble, a golden batch of drop biscuits welcomed us in the morning. We would enrich them with sweet tub butter, and dunk them into steaming cups of Café au Lait.

For evening desserts we had rice or bread puddings, and for Sundays and holidays, luscious pies like you wouldn't believe. My two favorites, which I could get Memere to prepare with a little coaxing, were her lemon meringue and her Creole coconut pies.

The following recipe is for the **CREOLE COCONUT PIE**. If you want to do it the easy way, you can begin with a store bought pie shell or make your crust with a prepared mix. But, mon ami, you'll know how a coconut pie should really taste if you start from scratch with Memere's recipe for the lightest, flakiest pie crust to ever melt "dans la Bouche Creole."

PASTRY SHELL

2 cups flour	**1 egg yolk**
½ tsp. salt	**2 tsp. sugar**
1⅓ sticks butter	**3 tbsp. cold water**

To make your pastry shell, first sift 2 cups flour with ½ tsp. salt into a bowl. Chop 1⅓ sticks of butter into small pieces and mix into the flour with your fingers. Keep mixing until the mixture looks like crumbs. Make a well in the center of the mixture and add 1 egg yolk, 2 teaspoons sugar, and 3 tablespoons cold water. Stir to combine all the ingredients and knead lightly with the fingers to form a smooth dough. (You may have to add another tablespoon of cold water.) Wrap the dough in wax paper or plastic and put in the refrigerator for ½ hour.

Roll the dough out on a floured board until it's about ⅛ inch thick. Roll it around the rolling pin, pick it up, and unroll it into your pie pan. Be sure to press down all around until the dough completely touches the bottom.

Bake the shell "blind." This means to bake without the filling. To prevent the shell from shrinking, line it with foil and then fill it with rice or dried beans. Put the shell into a 400-degree preheated oven for 10 minutes and then turn the heat down to 275°. Continue baking for 15 minutes longer. Remove the foil about halfway through the baking. Now you have a beautiful, golden brown pie crust into which you put the following filling. You'll need:

3 egg yolks	¼ cup cream
8 tbsp. sugar	1 cup shredded coconut
1 tbsp. cornstarch	1 tbsp. butter
¼ cup milk	2 tbsp. rum

Beat together the egg yolks and sugar until thick and light. Stir in the cornstarch. Mix the milk and cream and scald. Stir a little into the egg yolk mixture. When well mixed, add the rest and heat carefully, stirring constantly. Cook for 1 minute, or until thick and shiny. At this point, stir in the coconut, cook for about 1 minute longer, and then remove from the heat. Slice the butter into three or four pieces and mix this with the filling. Stir in the rum, pour the filling into the pie shell, and allow to cool.

MERINGUE

3 egg whites   **⅓ cup plus 2 tbsp. sugar**

Meanwhile, make a meringue with 3 egg whites and ⅓ cup sugar. Beat the egg whites until they peak and then beat in 2 tablespoons sugar. When this is well mixed, fold in the remaining sugar with a spoon. Pile this meringue high on the filling, being sure to seal it at the edges of the pastry shell.

Bake the pie in a 400-degree oven for 7 to 10 minutes until lightly browned. If you want to gild the lily, toast a tablespoon or two of shredded coconut and sprinkle it on top of the meringue. Let cool and satisfy your Bon Appetit!

PECAN PRALINES I

Supposedly, Marshal Duplesis-Preslin's (1598–1675) cook invented pralines. But millions of those crisp pecan goodies have been exported from New Orleans around the globe.

They are really not that difficult to make. Here's one way to prepare them.

1 cup brown sugar	**2 tbsp. butter**
1 cup white sugar	**¼ tsp. vanilla**
½ cup evaporated milk	**1 cup pecan halves**

Combine the sugar and milk and bring to a boil, stirring occasionally. Add the butter, pecans, and vanilla and cook until the syrup reaches the "soft ball stage" (238°). Cool without disturbing, then beat until somewhat thickened, but not until it loses its gloss. Drop by tablespoon onto a well-greased, flat surface. (A piece of marble is best for this.) The candy will flatten out into large cakes. Yield: 20 pralines.

Since there are many ways to prepare this delicacy, each with its own character and goodness, I include a couple more recipes for pecan pralines.

PECAN PRALINES II

1 cup granulated sugar
2 cups light brown sugar
3 tbsp. white corn syrup
⅛ tsp. salt

1¼ cups milk
1½ cups whole pecan
   halves
2 tsp. maple flavoring

Mix the sugars, corn syrup, salt, and milk in a saucepan. Heat to about 235° and cook, stirring constantly, until a little of the mixture forms a soft ball when dropped in cold water. Remove from heat and allow to cool to about lukewarm. Stir in the maple flavoring and the pecans; beat until the mixture begins to thicken. Drop quickly, a spoonful at a time, on waxed paper. When firm wrap in waxed paper.

PECAN PRALINES III

2 cups white sugar
1 cup brown sugar
1 stick butter

1 cup milk
2 tbsp. cane syrup
4 cups pecan halves

Mix the sugar, butter, milk, and cane syrup in a 3-quart saucepan and bring slowly to a boil, stirring constantly. Boil for 20 minutes, stirring occasionally. Add the pecan halves and continue to cook until the liquid forms a little ball when dropped into cold water. Stir well and drop by spoonfuls onto wax paper. The pralines will cool, congeal, and are then ready to be eaten.

CREAMY CREOLE PRALINES

¾ cup brown sugar
¾ cup white sugar
½ cup light cream

1 tbsp. butter
¼ tsp. maple flavor
1 cup pecan halves

Mix the sugar and cream together in a saucepan. Bring slowly to a boil. Lower the heat and continue cooking until a little of the mixture, when dropped in cold water, forms a soft ball. Remove from the heat and beat until the mixture is creamy. Add the butter, pecans and maple flavor (or substitute vanilla). Drop by spoonfuls on a buttered surface and allow to cool.

HOT LEMON PUFF

8 eggs, separated
1¼ cups sugar
1 tbsp. grated lemon rind

1 tsp. lemon extract
⅛ tsp. salt

Preheat the oven to 400°. Grease a 9-inch ovenproof casserole dish with butter.

Separate the eggs; place the yolks in the top of a double boiler and beat rapidly with a whisk until frothy. Add the sugar, lemon rind, and the extract and place over simmering water. Cook, stirring constantly, until the mixture is thick and smooth. Remove from heat.

Beat the egg whites with the salt until stiff and then fold gently and thoroughly into the yolk mixture. Pour into the buttered casserole. Place in the oven, turn the heat to 300°, and bake for 40 minutes or until firm and well puffed. It should be served hot.

PECAN CREAM CHEESE PIE

1 8-oz. pkg. Philadelphia
cream cheese
4 medium eggs
6 tbsp. sugar
2 tsp. vanilla

¾ cup corn syrup
1 cup pecans, finely
chopped
1 9-in pastry shell

Soften the cream cheese at room temperature. Cream together in a bowl with 1 egg, 4 tablespoons sugar, and 1 teaspoon vanilla. Keep stirring and beating until everything is well creamed with no lumps. In a separate bowl, beat together the corn syrup, 1 teaspoon vanilla, 3 eggs, and 2 tablespoons sugar.

Pour the cream cheese mixture into the pie shell. Level it off, and spread the chopped pecans on top. Pour over the pecans the mixture from the other bowl.

Bake in a preheated 375-degree oven for 35 minutes.

PECAN LACE COOKIES

1⅓ cups pecans, chopped
1 cup sugar
4 tbsp. flour
⅓ tsp. baking powder

dash of salt
1 stick of butter, melted
2 tsp. vanilla
1 egg, beaten

Mix together well the pecans, sugar, flour, baking powder, and salt. Add the melted butter, vanilla, and egg. Drop onto a cookie sheet in small ice teaspoon amounts. (Be sure the cookie sheet has been lined with kitchen parchment or aluminum foil.) Place about 3 inches apart.

Bake in a 325-degree oven for 8 to 12 minutes, depending upon your oven. Let cool. Peel off the parchment.

CRACKER PUDDING

1 qt. milk
2 eggs, separated
10 tbsp. sugar
2 cups coarsely broken
  soda crackers

1 cup shredded coconut
1 tsp. vanilla extract

Heat milk to lukewarm in a 3-quart saucepan. Beat the egg yolks, add sugar, and beat until well blended. Stir yolk mixture into warm milk. Add crackers and coconut. Simmer over medium heat, stirring occasionally, until thick, but not firm (about 10 minutes). Remove from heat. Beat the egg whites until stiff. Fold egg whites and vanilla into milk mixture. Put in refrigerator until chilled. To serve, sprinkle with toasted coconut. Serves six to eight.

FROZEN CREOLE CREAM CHEESE

5 cartons Creole cream
  cheese
1 qt. milk

1 qt. whipping cream
3 cups sugar
3 tsp. pure vanilla extract

Mash the cream cheese through a colander to eliminate large pieces. Add milk, whipping cream, and sugar; mix thoroughly. Add vanilla. Stir well, then put into the freezer. Tastes fantastic with fresh fruit.

PRALINE PARFAIT

¾ cup dark corn syrup
⅔ cup chopped pecans
⅓ cup dark molasses
5 tbsp. sugar
3 tbsp. boiling water

1 cup whipping cream
½ tsp. vanilla extract
1¼ pts. vanilla ice cream
⅓ cup pecan halves

Combine the corn syrup, chopped pecans, molasses, 3 tablespoons sugar, and boiling water in a 1½-quart saucepan. Bring to a boil. Remove from heat and cool. Whip the cream with the remaining 2 tablespoons sugar and the vanilla.

Alternately spoon ice cream and sauce into tall parfait glasses, ending with sauce. Top with whipped cream and garnish with pecan halves. Makes six servings.

PECAN DATE PIE

1 9-in. crust, unbaked
¾ cup butter
¾ cup brown sugar
2 egg yolks
½ cup evaporated milk

2 egg whites
¾ cup chopped pecans
1 cup chopped dates
⅛ tsp. powdered cloves
¼ tsp. cinnamon

Cream the butter, add sugar, and beat until creamy. Add the egg yolks one at a time. Blend in the milk, spices, pecans, and dates. Beat the egg whites until stiff and fold into the mixture.

Pour the mixture into pie crust and spread evenly. Bake 40 minutes at 350°. Serve with whipped cream.

PECAN PIE

1 8-in. pie shell, baked
⅓ cup butter
¾ cup firmly packed brown
   sugar
3 eggs

½ cup light corn syrup
1 cup chopped pecans
1 tsp. vanilla
¼ tsp. salt

Cream the butter and brown sugar. Beat in the eggs one at a time. Stir in the syrup, pecans, vanilla, and salt. Fill the pie shell with the mixture. Decorate the top with pecan halves, then bake at 375° for 30 minutes.

Ask any Creole the best way to make a cup of coffee, and without hesitation, he'll tell you how he does it. The Creoles described the coffee they drank as:

Noir comme le Diable
Fort comme la Mort
Doux comme l'amour
Et chaud comme l'enfer.

Freely translated, this meant they liked their coffee black as the devil, strong as death, sweet as love, and hot as Hades! No self-respecting Creole gentleman ever thrust a foot out of bed until he had had his morning cup of strong, hot, sweet black coffee. I remember as a small boy, sometimes Papete (my father) would give me a sip or two of his black coffee as I stood beside his bed.

Later, for breakfast, cups of Café au Lait were served. This was made by pouring hot coffee and boiling milk into the cup at the same time. After the coffee had been dripped, it was kept hot by putting the entire coffee pot into a large pot of hot water, and letting it simmer on the back of the stove. Never was the coffee ever reboiled. To do so would have ruined the taste for any discriminating coffee drinker.

Some observers swore that the Creoles dripped their coffee through an old sock! T'aint so, dear reader, t'aint so. What prompted this error was that small cloth bags were made that fit into the top section of the coffee pot. The dry coffee and chicory were spooned into the bag and the water poured over the coffee. Each household had a few of these bags, and when they were washed and hung out to dry on the line, they *did* resemble old socks! But oh, what wonderful tasting coffee they produced! Nowadays as I sometimes walk past the coffee stands in the French Market, I can't help but recall how often Mamete would fry up a batch of crisp beignets for our breakfast, for us to dunk into the steaming mugs of Café au Lait.

BEIGNETS

1 cup whole milk
2 tbsp. lard or shortening
2 tbsp. granulated sugar
1 pkg. dry yeast
3 cups all-purpose flour

1 tsp. ground nutmeg
1 tsp. salt
1 egg
oil for deep frying

Slowly heat the milk to the scalding point, stirring all the while. Put the shortening and the sugar in a bowl and then add the hot milk, stirring until the sugar and shortening are melted. Allow to cool to a lukewarm stage (no hotter than 100°). Pour in the yeast and stir until completely dissolved. Sift the flour, nutmeg, and salt together and gradually add about one half of the mixture to the milk to form a batter.

When the batter is smooth, add the egg and beat until well mixed. Add the rest of the flour mixture and stir until smooth. Cover with a towel and set aside to rise.

In about an hour the dough will have doubled in volume. At this point, knead gently and place on a floured board. Roll out to about ¼ inch thickness.

Cut into diamond shapes with a sharp knife and cover with a towel for about 45 minutes, so the dough will rise. Heat the oil to 385°. (Check with a thermometer.)

Fry the beignets. (Try to turn them only once.) When they are a beautiful golden brown, drain on paper and dust with powdered sugar.

A real treat with Café au Lait for your Bon Appetit!

CREOLE HONEY CAKE

2 sticks butter
1 cup honey
4 eggs, beaten
1 tbsp. lemon juice
1 tsp. grated lemon rind
3 cups sifted all-purpose
   flour

2 tbsp. baking powder
½ tsp. salt
¾ cup chopped pecans
1 cup citron or any glazed
   fruit

Melt the butter and mix well with the honey. Add the eggs, lemon juice, and grated lemon rind. Mix well and slowly add the sifted flour, baking powder, and salt. Blend thoroughly but do not over mix. Chop the citron and pecans and blend in the mixture. Pour into a pan lined with wax paper and bake in a 350-degree oven for about 1 hour.

I usually like to describe Creole cooking in two words, elegant and economical. Eye as well as taste appeal motivated those old Creole cooks. When Memere fixed a dish of chitterlings, red beans and rice, wild rabbit in sauce piquante, or a hogshead cheese, the manner in which it was served was as important as the way it was made.

As for economy, Memere and Mamete never wasted a thing. For example, their hashes were works of art. They were made from the soup meat left over from the previous evening meal. And what they did with stale bread was incredible. If the bread wasn't too stale, it would be sprinkled lightly with water and put in the oven for a few minutes. It came out hot and crisp. For a variation, butter and blue cheese (equal amounts would be mixed together), and a tablespoon of finely chopped onions would be spread over the sliced bread and allowed to melt in the oven.

We had two bread receptacles in our kitchen, a bread box and a bread bag. The bread box kept the bread fresh. It had been delivered earlier in the morning and was put in the airtight bread box. Any bread left over in the evening was put in the bread bag. The bread bag was a long white cloth bag with a drawstring at the top. If bread crumbs were needed to panée meat or sprinkle on any food, pieces were taken out and rolled with a rolling pin.

Once or twice a week, if the stale bread began to pile up, we'd have a breakfast of "pain perdu," or lost bread. The bread was sliced about an inch thick and allowed to soak a few minutes in a mixture of 2 beaten eggs, 1 cup milk, ½ cup sugar, and ½ teaspoon vanilla extract. The slices were then gently fried in oil until they were brown on both sides. Before being served, they were lightly sprinkled with powdered sugar.

If there was any quantity of bread left over by the weekend, this was made into a pudding and sometimes served with a delicious whiskey sauce poured over it.

BREAD PUDDING I

1 loaf stale bread (the more stale, the better)
1 qt. milk
4 eggs
2 cups sugar
2 tbsp. pure vanilla extract
1 cup seedless raisins
2 apples, peeled, cored, and sliced
¼ cup butter

Crush the bread into the milk and mix well. Beat the eggs and add to the bread and milk, together with the sugar, vanilla, raisins, and apples. Mix well. Melt the butter and pour into the pan in which you're going to bake the pudding, then pour in the rest of the ingredients.

Bake about 50 minutes in a preheated 350-degree oven (until the pudding is firm). This can be served when cool as is, or with the whiskey sauce.

WHISKEY SAUCE

½ cup melted butter
1 cup sugar
1 egg, beaten
whiskey to taste

Cream the butter and sugar in a double boiler. Add the egg and stir rapidly, so the egg doesn't curdle. When well mixed, allow to cool. Add whiskey to taste (a jigger or two). Bon Appetit!

Here's another variation on the old bread pudding theme.

BREAD PUDDING II

1 loaf French bread
3 cups whole milk
4 medium cooking apples,
   peeled, cored, and sliced
   thin
10 pitted prunes, chopped
¾ box raisins (8.8 oz.)
4 eggs
1 can sliced peaches (29
   oz.)
1½ tbsp. vanilla
¾ tsp. powdered nutmeg
⅓ tsp. cinnamon
1 stick butter
1 cup sugar

Heat the milk just to the boiling point. (Do not boil.) Pour warm milk over crumbled French bread; mix well until all bread pieces are soaked in milk. Set bread and milk mixture aside.

Grease a large mixing bowl (Pyrex) with butter, making sure all surface of bowl is coated. Break 4 eggs into the greased bowl, then add the canned peaches. Beat the egg and peach mixture until eggs are well blended. Add 1 cup sugar and stir well. Add vanilla, nutmeg, cinnamon, sliced apples, chopped prunes, and raisins while stirring well. After the mixture is well blended, cut 10 thin slices from the stick of butter and stir into mixture. Add the milk-soaked bread and mix very well.

Bake in a preheated oven at 350° for 1 hour and 15 minutes. Allow to cool until pudding becomes firm.

CUSTARD SAUCE

1 egg
½ cup sugar
1 tsp. cornstarch
½ cup milk
½ cup cream
3 tbsp. rum

Beat egg and sugar together over low fire. Dissolve the cornstarch in milk and cream. Beat into the eggs and sugar. Bring to a short boil, then turn flame low. Stir constantly with whisk until thick. Add rum. This is delicious served over your bread pudding.

ZABAGLIONE

3 tbsp. sugar   3 egg yolks
3 tbsp. sherry

Mix the sugar, sherry, and egg yolks together. Cook very carefully in a double boiler with water at a simmer. Stir the mixture constantly until it thickens almost to a paste. Serve hot over bread pudding.

BANANAS FOSTER

3 bananas   1 tsp. vanilla
1 stick butter   ½ cup rum
1 cup brown sugar (You may   ½ cup banana liqueur
   add ½ tsp. cinnamon if
   desired.)

Slice the bananas in 3 slices lengthwise, then cut in halves. Melt the butter in a skillet or frying pan, add brown sugar, and cook over low heat, stirring into a thick paste. Add vanilla and banana liqueur and stir well. Cook about 3 minutes. Add banana slices and cook over medium heat, basting well with the sugar and butter mixture. Cook about 5 minutes. (Mixture will bubble while cooking.)

Heat the rum in a metal cup, ignite, and pour over bananas. (Rum will have faint blue flame in cup and will flame up when poured over the bananas.) Stir well to blend, then serve the mixture with pieces of bananas over vanilla ice cream.

BUTTERSCOTCH PIE

½ stick butter
¼ cup all-purpose flour
2 cups milk
2 egg yolks, beaten
1 cup sugar
1 tbsp. pure vanilla extract

1 9-in. pie shell, baked
   according to directions
½ pt. whipping cream
2 tbsp. confectioners sugar
2 tbsp. brandy

Melt 2 tablespoons of the butter in a heavy skillet over low heat. Stir in the flour. Cook, stirring, for about 3 minutes. Slowly add the milk, stir, and bring to a boil. Let it simmer over low heat. Melt the remaining butter in another heavy pot or skillet, add the sugar, and cook over medium heat, stirring constantly, until the sugar turns a light brown. Pour into the hot flour sauce and continue to stir over low heat until the mixture is smooth. Remove from the heat and stir in the beaten egg yolks and vanilla. If there should be tiny lumps, pour through a strainer. Let the mixture cool, then pour into the baked pastry shell.

Pour the whipping cream into a bowl and whip until it peaks. Mix in the confectioners sugar and the brandy. Top the pie with the cream and chill until ready to serve. This will serve six to eight.

RAISIN BUTTERSCOTCH PIE

CRUST

½ cup finely chopped
   pecans
½ cup softened butter
¾ cup finely chopped
   raisins

4 tbsp. brown sugar
1 cup sifted flour

Put all of the ingredients together, and stir until very well mixed. Pour the mixture into a 9-inch pie pan and press around the sides and bottom to form a crust. Stick the bottom with a fork a number of times and then bake at 375° for about 10 minutes or until lightly browned. Set aside.

FILLING

1 cup brown sugar	2 tbsp. butter
6 tbsp. cornstarch	2 tsp. vanilla
1½ cups light cream	1 tsp. almond extract
½ tsp. salt	1 cup chopped raisins
3 egg yolks	1 cup sour cream

Mix the brown sugar in a pan along with the salt and cornstarch. Stir in the cream. Put the pan over a low to moderate heat and cook, stirring constantly, until the mixture begins to thicken. Lower the heat and continue cooking until very thick. (This should take about 15 minutes.) The mixture needs stirring only occasionally. Remove from the heat and beat in the egg yolks one at a time; allow to cook over low heat 5 minutes longer. Remove from the heat and beat in the butter, vanilla, and almond extract. When well mixed, stir in the raisins and allow to cool to about lukewarm. Stir in the sour cream and pour into the pie shell. Top with meringue.

MERINGUE

3 egg whites	
pinch of salt	6 tbsp. sugar

Beat the egg whites until foamy. Add the salt and continue to beat until the mixture forms soft peaks. Gradually add the sugar until it is completely dissolved. Beat the meringue until stiff peaks form. Pour over the pie.

Preheat the oven to 400°. Bake the pie for 8 to 10 minutes, or until the meringue peaks become slightly browned. This pie should be completely cool before cutting.

APPLE CREAM CHEESE PIE

1 9 in. pastry shell
1½ cups peeled and thinly
  sliced fresh apples
¾ cup sugar
¼ tsp. cinnamon
¼ tsp. nutmeg
⅛ tsp. salt
2 eggs, beaten
½ cup cream
6 ozs. Philadelphia cream
  cheese
1 tsp. vanilla

Mix together the apple slices, ¼ cup of the sugar, cinnamon, and nutmeg and arrange in the pastry shell. Bake in a preheated 450-degree oven for 15 minutes. Remove from the oven and turn the heat down to 325°.

Cream together the remaining ½ cup sugar, the salt, and the cream cheese. (If the cheese is allowed to soften it will cream much easier.) Add the eggs and mix until smooth. Add to this the cream and vanilla and mix well. Pour over the apples in the pie shell and bake in the 325-degree oven for 40 minutes.

CREAM CHEESE CUSTARD PIE

2 8-oz. and 1 6-oz. pkg.
  Philadelphia cream
  cheese
1¼ cups sugar
2 tbsp. cornstarch
1 pinch salt
4 eggs
1 tbsp. vanilla
1 tbsp. lemon juice
2 tbsp. milk
2 tbsp. sour cream
2 graham cracker pie crusts

Let the cream cheese soften at room temperature. Mix together the sugar, cornstarch, and salt. When the cream cheese is soft, combine the sugar mixture a little at a time with the cream cheese; beat until well mixed. Beat the eggs and add to the cheese mixture. When well mixed, add the milk, sour cream, vanilla, and lemon juice. Pour the mixture into the pie shells and bake in a pan of water, in a preheated 350-degree oven, for 1¼ hours.

Refrigerate about 1 hour before serving. You may, if you wish, top with whipped cream before serving.

YVETTE'S LEMON PIE

3 egg yolks
1 cup sugar
2 tbsp. all-purpose flour
¼ cup melted butter
¼ cup strained lemon juice
1 tbsp. finely grated lemon
　rind

¾ cup milk
1 cup sour cream
1 9-in. pie crust (can be
　graham cracker)

Pour the egg yolks into a double boiler and beat with a whisk for a minute or so. Add the sugar, flour, melted butter, lemon juice, and lemon rind; mix well. (Keep the water boiling in the double boiler.) Blend in the milk and cook about 15 minutes, stirring constantly, until the mixture thickens. Allow the filling to cool and then fold in the sour cream. Mix well and pour into the pie crust. Now prepare the meringue.

MERINGUE

3 large egg whites
¼ tsp. cream of tartar
1 tbsp. water

6 tbsp. sugar
⅛ tsp. salt
2 tsp. pure vanilla extract

First, clean the bowl very well and dry thoroughly. Beat the egg whites, cream of tartar, and water on the high speed of the electric mixer for about 3 minutes or until the whites begin to stand in peaks. Add the sugar, 1 tablespoon at a time, then add the salt and vanilla. Continue beating until whites are stiff. Pile lightly on the filled pie crust and bake in a preheated 325-degree oven for 15 to 20 minutes or until meringue is brown. Wait until the pie is cool before cutting. Will serve six to eight.

STRAWBERRY CHEESECAKE

25 graham crackers
1 stick butter
1 3-oz. pkg. Philadelphia
   cream cheese, softened at
   room temperature
1 cup sugar

3 eggs, beaten
1 8-oz. carton sour cream
1 pkg. strawberry jello
1 pkg. frozen, sliced
   strawberries
1 cup water

Crush the graham crackers with a rolling pin into fine crumbs. Melt the butter and mix with the crumbs until the crumbs are all moistened. Line a 9-inch by 9-inch square cake pan with the mixture, both bottom and sides. Mix the sugar and cream cheese until creamy. Add the beaten eggs and mix well with a spoon. Pour into the crust and bake at 350° for 30 minutes. Stir the sour cream until smooth and pour over the baked cream cheese mixture; return to the oven to bake 20 minutes at 350°. Set aside until cold.

Dissolve the jello in 1 cup of boiling water. Mix in the frozen strawberries and gently pour into the baked cake. Cover this with foil and place in the refrigerator for at least 8 hours or preferably overnight. Cut into squares to serve.

PAIN PATATE (YAM PUDDING)

2½ lbs. yams or sweet
   potatoes
2½ sticks butter
2 cups all-purpose flour
1 tsp. baking powder
1½ tsp. freshly ground
   nutmeg

½ tsp. cinnamon
½ tsp. salt
1½ cups light brown sugar
4 eggs
½ cup milk
2 tsp. pure vanilla

Literally translated, "Pain Patate" means yam bread.

Place the yams into enough boiling water to cover them and boil until tender; drain. Allow to cool, then peel and mash. With a piece of the butter, grease a 13- by 10- by 2-inch baking dish. Preheat the oven to 375°.

Combine the flour, baking powder, cinnamon, nutmeg, and salt in a bowl and then sift. Cream the butter and the sugar together in another bowl until it is light and fluffy. Beat the eggs in one at a time. Add about half of the flour mixture, then half of the milk and mix thoroughly. Add the rest of the flour and milk and again mix thoroughly. Stir in the mashed yams and the vanilla. Pour the mixture into the greased baking dish and bake in the middle of the oven for about 45 minutes. When the top is golden brown the pudding is ready and should be eaten at once. Serves six to eight.

RICE FRITTERS

1 cup cooked rice
2 eggs
2 tbsp. raisins
¼ tsp. grated lemon rind
2 tbsp. chopped almonds

2 tsp. baking powder
3 tbsp. flour
powdered sugar
oil

Combine rice, eggs, raisins, lemon rind, almonds, flour, and baking powder. Heat oil at a depth of about 2 inches in a heavy skillet until a bit of the mixture when dropped in the oil fries and browns in about 40 seconds. Use a tablespoon to drop the mixture into the hot oil. When brown on one side, turn over. When brown on both sides, remove, drain on paper toweling, and sprinkle with powdered sugar. Can be served with maple syrup, jam, or jelly.

RICE PUDDING

I ve described Creole cooking as both elegant and economical. The Creoles never wasted anything. When there was rice left over from the previous day's meal, they either ate it for breakfast with milk and sugar or had it that evening as a RICE PUDDING. However, if you're starting from scratch, do it this way.

1 cup uncooked rice	½ cup raisins
1 qt. milk	5 eggs, beaten
8 tbsp. butter	1 tsp. grated lemon rind
¾ cup sugar	1 tsp. cinnamon
1 tsp. vanilla	

Combine rice and milk. Bring to a boil, cover, and cook over low heat until rice is tender. Add the butter, sugar, vanilla, lemon rind, raisins, and eggs. Pour into a buttered 2-quart casserole dish. Sprinkle with the cinnamon and bake at 350° for about 25 minutes. This will serve between six and eight.

CALAS

6 tbsp. flour	pinch nutmeg
3 heaping tbsp. sugar	2 cups cooked rice
2 tsp. baking powder	2 eggs
¼ tsp. salt	cooking oil
¼ tsp. vanilla	powdered sugar

Mix together the flour, sugar, baking powder, salt, vanilla, and nutmeg. Beat the eggs and rice. Add the dry ingredients to the rice and egg mixture. When thoroughly mixed, drop by spoonfuls into hot, deep fat (about 360°) and fry until brown. Drain on paper towel. Sprinkle with powdered sugar and serve while hot.

index